CENTERING PRAYER

Centering Prayer

Renewing an Ancient
Christian Prayer Form

M. Basil Pennington, O.C.S.O.

Doubleday & Company, Inc.
Garden City, New York
1980

Grateful acknowledgment is made to the following for permission to use previously copyrighted material:

Excerpts from The Jerusalem Bible, copyright © 1966 by Darton, Longman & Todd, Ltd., and Doubleday & Company, Inc. Used by permission of the publisher.

Excerpts from *The Cloud of Unknowing and the Book of Privy Counseling*, newly edited, with an Introduction by William Johnston, Copyright © 1973 by William Johnston, Image Books. Reprinted by permission of Doubleday & Company, Inc.

Excerpts from "Conference of Mother Alexandra," from *In Search of True Wisdom: Visits to Eastern Spiritual Fathers* by Sergius Bolshakoff and M. Basil Pennington, O.C.S.O., Copyright © 1979 by Cistercian Abbey of Spencer, Inc. Reprinted by permission of Doubleday & Company, Inc.

Excerpts from *Time and Myth* by John S. Dunne, Copyright © 1973 by John S. Dunne. Reprinted by permission of Doubleday & Company, Inc.

Excerpts from *The Climate of Monastic Prayer* by Thomas Merton. Cistercian Publications. 1969.

Excerpts from the following works by William of St. Thierry: *The Nature of Body and Soul, On Prayer, Meditation, On the Nature and Dignity of Love, Mirror of Faith*. Cistercian Publications. 1971.

ISBN: 0-385-14562-4
Library of Congress Catalog Card Number: 78-22348
Copyright © 1980 by Cistercian Abbey of Spencer, Inc.
Printed in the United States of America

DEDICATION

To
Dom M. Edmund Futterer, O.C.S.O.

Founder and first abbot of
Saint Joseph's Abbey, Spencer

Propagator of the
Cistercian Order
in South America

A great and wise spiritual father
on the occasion of the
golden jubilee of his
monastic profession
1929–79

Out of his infinite glory,
may he give you the power through his Spirit
for your hidden self to grow strong,
so that Christ may live in your hearts through faith,
and then,
planted in love and built on love,
you will with all the saints have strength
to grasp the breadth and the length,
the height and the depth;
until, knowing the love of Christ,
which is beyond all knowledge,
you are filled with the utter fullness of God.

—Ep. 3:16–19

CONTENTS

INTRODUCTION

"I want to pray." I think that is basically the life statement that leads one to open a book like this. What leads each particular person to such a statement, expressed or unexpressed, is quite personal and comes out of a life being lived and the influences that have been forming the attitudes and values that guide that life.

For some, and I suspect they are in the minority today, such a statement is motivated by a sense of duty. We have been taught that this is what a decent person does. It is the Creator's due. Life is somehow not all put together without the element of prayer. In more and more lives this sense of duty is underpinned by a real sense of need. There is an incompleteness, an inability to cope with or adequately respond to life's demands. It may be more in relation to others. Men and women in ministry sense their shallowness or lack of really significant response to the naked and pained need of those to whom they minister, those who turn to them for help. Parents sense that Christian teaching, Christian morality, Christian hope, are the elements that will best help their children negotiate the vicissitudes that lie ahead or presently face them. Yet they are at a loss how to pass these on effectively to the emerging persons they so dearly love.

Many a friend knows the compassionate pain of not being able to bring a missing insight, a sense of value and worth, a hope, to where it is sorely needed. We sense a need to fall back on prayer.

The needs of others, which duty or love or both demand we experience in some way as our own, do nudge us or even compel us to be in touch with our own needs—needs that are in fact very much the same. There surface in us if we dare leave enough space in our rush-rush lives to allow it, or if circumstances, as they often do, trap us in a situation where we can't avoid it, some of our own needs—above all, perhaps, our loneliness, our incompleteness, our lacks, our inability to be and to do what we want.

Whatever it is that evokes in us the statement or the cry: "I want to pray," we do want and need practical help to respond. And we know that the mere repetition of words, however beautiful, is not going to fill the bill. The cry comes from some deeper, some very deep part of our being, and we need to get in touch with that center and let our prayer arise from there. Ideally we should be able to turn to parent, pastor, or Christian friend and say: "Teach me how to pray, to meditate, to experience God." But unfortunately we sense or know as we look about us that there is no one to whom we can confidently address this simple request with a solid hope of receiving practical and satisfying help. At least that has been the experience of many. True renewal is under way within the Christian community. More and more, we can find at hand someone to whom we can confidently address such a request. Yet this is still far from being universally true. And that is why there is still a need for such books as this and why this book has been written.

In seeking to share this very simple form of prayer that has been a constant part of our Christian tradition, I have endeavored to be very practical and concrete. I have gone into details; I have at times stated the obvious. I have tried to answer all the questions that I have heard arise in workshops over the years, that have come to me in letters, that have been raised in counseling sessions or during discussions—the simplest as well as the more sophisticated and complex. (This is not to say that new questions will not continue to arise. Each reader will have his or her own—though if he or she rereads the book with the new questions in mind, the answers might well be found.) The endeavor has been to make it possible for the reader to enter into the practice of this prayer with a certain confidence and sense of security. It certainly is my hope and prayer that for each reader this will not be a book that is only read, but one that is put into practice.

Our practice, our prayer, must be a response to reality, to what truly is. The factor that has perhaps most undermined the spiritual life of the Western Christian Church has been the divorce between theology and spirituality, between doctrine and practice. So, in the course of speaking about prayer and sharing a very practical method of prayer, I do not hesitate to recur to even the most profound mysteries of our Christian faith. Yet I have tried to maintain a certain conciseness so that the riches of our faith are certainly not fully explored or developed but are presented in quite seminal form. The particular theological expression I employ may not be familiar to some of my readers. This will probably be so not because it is a peculiarly Catholic expression or comes from a particular school of theology but because it is a more traditional and ancient expression found in the Fathers, one all too often neglected and unknown in our times. I hope the reader will have patience with me in this and perhaps through it come to some new insights into our faith which will ground a fuller and richer practice and experience.

The author of *The Cloud of Unknowing* felt the need in his Introduction (and he states it again near the end of his treatise) to implore the reader to read the whole of his dense little work, fearing that if only parts are read they will convey an incomplete or even false understanding. I am sensing something of the same need. The matter is delicate and in some ways complex, for it involves a very full and deep relationship between two persons: a human person whose potential is limitless, and the infinite God. Especially in the responses to the questions will the reader find nuances and distinctions that can be quite helpful and, for some, very important. This is the great value of being able to take part in a workshop. Through succeeding experiences of Centering Prayer and the responses to the questions arising from such experience, teaching can be honed to meet the need each one has for an adequate understanding to support his or her practice.

This is what I am interested in: to facilitate and support the entrance into and regular practice of contemplative prayer. I am not trying to meet and respond to all the objections of critics. Above all, I am not interested in any polemics. Nor do I have any desire to teach or affirm the supremacy of one form of prayer over another. I simply want to share a gift I have received with all those who are interested and are drawn by God's merciful love to share it with me.

I think I can make the words of the author of *The Cloud* my own:

> Should it seem that the way of prayer I have described in this book is unsuited to you spiritually or temperamentally, feel perfectly free to leave it aside and with wise counsel seek another in full confidence. In that case I trust you will hold me excused for all I have written here. Truly, I wrote only according to my simple understanding of these things and with no other purpose than that of helping you. So read it over two or three times. The more often you read it the better, for that much more will you grasp its meaning. Parts that seemed difficult and obscure at first may perhaps become obvious and clear as you read it again.
>
> It seems to me that anyone whom grace has drawn to contemplation will not read this book (or hear it read) without feeling that it speaks of something akin to his own spirit. Should you feel this way and find it helpful, thank God with all your heart and for love of him pray for me. (Ch. 74, pp. 143–44)

I very much want to express my sincere gratitude to my abbot, Father Thomas Keating, and to my confrere Father William Meninger. Much of what I share here comes from them. They have very generously read over the manuscript and offered much good advice for its improvement. Many who have taken part in workshops with me over the years have made their contributions and I am grateful to them, also. Above all, it is the prayerful support of my community and many others that bears this fruit. Most especially must I mention that little Benedictine nun who spent many hours at her typewriter and more at her prie-dieu bringing this book to life. She prefers to remain incognito, so I count on the Lord himself to reward her and her sisters who have supported her in this work. With humble gratitude.

Easter, 1979   *M. Basil*

CENTERING PRAYER

IT'S BEYOND US—YET OURS

I would like to start this book with a word from Scripture—in this way I can be sure that something worthwhile will have been said. As we read the Scriptures day in and day out over the years, various passages speak to us with special force. Some come to be particularly meaningful and we return to them again and again. One such passage for me is the following from Saint Paul's First Letter to the Corinthians:

> The hidden wisdom of God which we teach in our mysteries is the wisdom that God predestined to be for our glory before the ages began. . . . we teach what scripture calls: *the things that no eye has seen and no ear has heard, things beyond the mind of man, all that God has prepared for those who love him.*
>
> These are the very things God has revealed to us through the Spirit, for the Spirit reaches the depths of everything, even the depths of God. After all, the depths of a man can only be known by his own spirit, not by any other man, and in the same way the depths of God can only be known by the Spirit of God. Now instead of the spirit of the world, we have received the Spirit that comes from God, to teach us to understand the gifts that he has given us. Therefore we teach, not in the way in which philosophy is taught, but in the way that the Spirit teaches us; we teach spiritual things spiritually. An unspiritual person is one who does not accept

anything of the Spirit of God: he sees it all as nonsense; it is beyond his understanding because it can only be understood by means of the Spirit. A spiritual man, on the other hand, is able to judge the value of everything, and his own value is not to be judged by other men. As scripture says: *Who can know the mind of the Lord . . . ?* But we are those who have the mind of Christ. (1 Co. 2:7,9–16)

This is essentially what we are going to be sharing in this book: "The hidden wisdom of God . . . the wisdom that God predestined to be for our glory before the ages began . . . *that no eye has seen and no ear has heard, things beyond the mind of man, all that God has prepared for those who love him, . . .*" what he "has revealed to us through the Spirit."

In Centering Prayer we go beyond thought and image, beyond the senses and the rational mind, to that center of our being where God is working a wonderful work. There God our Father is not only bringing us forth at each moment in his wonderful creative love, but by virtue of the grace of filiation, which we received at baptism, he is indeed making us sons and daughters, one with his own Son, pouring out in our hearts the Spirit of his Son, so that we can in fullest sense cry, "*Abba*, Father." He says to us, in fact more than in word: "You are my son; this day have I begotten you." At this level of our being, where we are our truest selves, we are essentially prayer, total response to the Father in our oneness with the Son, in that love who is the Holy Spirit. This is the mystery hidden from the ages—the great design of an eternal, loving Providence—and revealed to us. As the Son said to us in the Upper Room: "I no longer call you servants, but friends, because I have made known to you all that the Father has made known to me. . . . You cannot understand now. . . . But the Spirit, the Paraclete, the Comforter, the Strengthener—whom the Father will send in my name, will teach you everything and remind you of all I have said to you."

"These are the very things God has revealed to us through the Spirit. . . . An unspiritual person [one who does not have the Holy Spirit] is one who does not accept anything of the Spirit of God: he sees it all as nonsense." Indeed, without faith, without the powerful action of the Holy Spirit, Centering Prayer is just so much *nonsense!* Just sitting there, doing nothing. Not even thinking some worthwhile thoughts, or making some good resolutions—just *being*. Unless we are in touch with who we really are, "just being" seems hardly enough. "The depths of a man can only be known by his own spirit." True enough. But we are not men only. We have been baptized into Christ, we have been transformed, deified, in some way made one with the very Son of God, and partakers of the divine nature. And so it is only through the Holy Spirit, who "reaches the depths of everything, even the depths of God," that we can hope to understand what "can only be understood by means of the Spirit." "We teach spiritual things spiritually,"—that is, in and by the Holy Spirit.

As you begin this book on Centering Prayer I would like to encourage you to stop for a bit and turn to the Holy Spirit, dwelling within you. He is *your* Spirit, the Gift given to you at baptism to be your very own spirit; ask him through the words printed on these pages to "teach spiritual things spiritually." And as you move through the pages, may you be constantly aware of his presence, opening out to you something of the full beauty of who you really are and gently inviting you to enjoy that beauty, to wonder at it, to live out of its fullness.

Centering Prayer, under one aspect, is but a very simple method —a technique, if you like that term—to get in touch with what *is*. But its practice is surely not meant just to enliven forty minutes of our day. It is meant to open the way to living constantly out of the center, to living out of the fullness of who we are.

This is certainly something sublime, wondrous, beyond all our human expectations. "Eye has not seen, nor ear heard, nor has it entered into the heart of man." Yet it is to this that we are *all* called.

Let me share with you another favorite Scripture passage. This one is from the last book in the Bible, the Book of Revelation, Chapter Three:

> Here is the message of the Amen, the faithful, the true witness, the ultimate source of God's creation: I know all about you: how you are neither cold nor hot. I wish you were one or the other, but since

you are neither, but only lukewarm, I will spit you out of my mouth. You say to yourself, "I am rich, I have made a fortune, and have everything I want," never realizing that you are wretchedly and pitiably poor, and blind and naked too. I warn you, buy from me the gold that has been tested in the fire to make you really rich, and white robes to clothe you and cover your shameful nakedness, and eye ointment to put on your eyes so that you are able to see. I am the one who reproves and disciplines all those he loves, so repent in real earnest. Look, I am standing at the door, knocking. If one of you hears me calling and opens the door, I will come in to share his meal, side by side with him. Those who prove victorious I will allow to share my throne, just as I was victorious myself and took my place with my Father on his throne. If anyone has ears to hear, let him listen to what the Spirit is saying to the churches." (Rv. 3:14–22)

There is in this passage one of the most frightening words which our Lord speaks to us: "I know all about you" (I've got your number); "you are neither cold nor hot." How true! We are not cold, indifferent, turned off—or we wouldn't be reading a book like this. Yet, on the other hand, who of us will dare to say he is really "hot" —burning with the fire of divine love? We have only to allow the briefest moment's reflection on our actual performance, our backsliding, our compromises, our rationalizations, our sin. And what is our blessed Lord's reaction to all this? He is graphically frank: "Since you are neither hot nor cold, but only lukewarm, I will spit you out of my mouth"—or, as another translation would have it: "vomit you forth from my mouth." Our Lord, who was so totally a "yes" to the Father, whose sacred heart did indeed burn with love and filial devotion, can only feel the deepest disgust toward our lukewarmness. When he sees the way we respond to the constant goodness of divine Love, it quite simply makes him feel like vomiting. That is how disgusting we, in all our pettiness, meanness, selfishness, really are. Our Lord has certainly called our number.

And yet!—and this is the sublimity of this word of the Lord, this message of life and hope, to the very ones whom he so rightly finds so disgusting—our Lord, overcoming, as it were, his natural repugnance and knowing the full power of his own immense love to enflame our lukewarmness, goes on to say: "Look, I am standing at the door, knocking." In spite of all our lukewarmness, our inattentiveness, our deafness, he never tires, never ceases to seek to enter into our lives.

In spite of all this, he who made us, who has every right over us, profoundly respects us, as no one else so fully does. He knows the greatest thing about us is our freedom, our power to choose, to love. Therein, precisely, lies our particular likeness to the divine. And he will never violate that freedom, no matter how sadly we choose to abuse it. He will never force his way into our lives: "Behold, I am standing at the door, knocking. *If one of you hears me . . . and opens. . . .*" He humbly waits, till we open. And that is all we have to do: just open to him, and he will do the rest. No matter how disgusting we are. No matter what our track record has been. We have but to open and he will come in. This is his word, expressed unconditionally, to those whose lukewarmness he knows full well. Centering Prayer is but a simple way to open the door— wide—all the way—to let him come in.

"I will come in to share his meal, side by side with him." With a concreteness, a warmth, a full humanness, our Lord expresses the intimacy he wants to share with each one of us. The most common sign of human friendship is to sit down together and share a meal. But the intimacy here is special: a meal just for two—"If *one* of you hears me . . ." and we won't sit with a table between us. It will be "side by side"—like the beloved disciple, who could lean over and rest his head upon his Master's bosom. We are in the last pages of the Revelation, and our Lord harks back to the first, at the dawn of creation, when he made man, and in the cool of the evening came down and walked arm in arm with him under the shade of the trees. God made man to be his intimate friend; that is the message woven through the whole of Scripture. *All* are called to the intimacy of contemplative union with God, not just a chosen few. Not just the paragons of virtue, but even we poor, disgusting, lukewarm, backsliding sinners!

We are called to intimacy, indeed to union! Here, continuing to use very graphic imagery, our Lord tells us: "Those who prove victorious [not a great victory on our part—we have but to open a door —but thus we gratuitously receive as our own the fullness of his great victory] I will allow to share my throne, just as I was victorious myself and took my place with my Father on his throne." Our Lord is expressing here the fulfillment, in concrete imagery, of his earnest priestly prayer, "May they all be one, Father, as you are in me and I am in you, may they be one in us." We are summoned not only to intimacy but to take possession of our very oneness with the Son of God in the inner life of the Trinity in the communication of the very Love of Father and Son, the Most Holy Spirit. This is what Centering Prayer is all about.

William of Saint Thierry, a great twelfth-century spiritual father, about whom we will say more later, expresses this most beautifully. And—this I want to point out—he expresses it not in one of his sublime treatises on mystical theology but in a very basic work in which, with the help of pagan doctors and philosophers as well as Fathers of the Church ("I have gathered together here what I have found in the books of philosophers and physicians, and also in ecclesiastical writers"), he tries to set forth quite simply *The Nature of the Body and the Soul* and the full significance of God's creative and recreative work therein. His words, then, are clearly applicable to any human person who has or is a body and soul:

> For just as the body lives from the soul, so does the soul live from God. . . . It lives as one spirit with him. For the Will of the Father and the Son—the Holy Spirit, by an inconceivable grace, with unutterable joy, by most secret inspiration, in a most manifest operation, conforms the will of the soul to himself, uniting its love to himself with spiritual omnipotence. He becomes so united with the soul that, as has been said, when the soul prays with aspirations beyond conception, it is rather the Spirit who is said to pray. And this is the prayer of the Son to the Father: "I will [that is, I bring it about by the power of my will which is the Holy Spirit] that as I and you are one in substance, so they also may be one in us through grace." One in love, one in beatitude, one in immortality and incorruption, and

even in some way in divinity itself. For "to as many as received him he gave the power to become sons of God."

What we are called to is indeed far beyond us, and yet in virtue of our baptism it is already ours. We need but appropriate it and enjoy it. And that is the "work" of Centering Prayer.

II

A GIFT FROM THE DESERT

We tend to think of our own times as being unique in the history of the human family, and in some ways that is certainly true. And yet there is undeniable truth in the words of the Wise Man: ". . . there is nothing new under the sun" (Qo. 1:9).

In recent years, we have seen a significant number of young and not so young Westerners turning to the East. Though the tide seems now to have ebbed, there was for a time a steady flow of pilgrims seeking from gurus, swamis, and roshis some sampling of ancient wisdom. Some actually made the long journey to Benares, Sri Lanka, or Thailand. Others were able to import masters or find them already imported, or in some cases even satisfied themselves with what returning disciples were able to share.

This phenomenon of dropping out of one's own life current, whether it be school or business or religious-community life, and heading toward the East in search of wisdom is not unprecedented. It was very much present in the renewal of the eleventh and twelfth centuries, finding fearsome and dramatic expression in the Crusades but significant peaceful expression in the realms of art, science, and sapiential literature. This was the period when Peter the Venerable translated the Koran, and the writings of many of the Greek Fathers were first made available in Latin, thus directly influencing the evolution of spiritual thinking in Western Europe.

The fourth and fifth centuries also witnessed such a movement.

My own patron, Basil—later called "the Great"—and his schoolmate Gregory, the Theologian, threw aside their books, left the prestigious schools of Athens, and went off to find true wisdom among the *gerontas* (old men) in Syria and Egypt; "old man" is a term of respect used even today among the Greeks to address or speak about a significant spiritual father. St. Jerome might truly be included among these seekers, as well as his friends Paula and Melania, the Elder and the Younger. Among the pilgrims to the East must also be included a brilliant young man from Dalmatia whom the Eastern Christians today call St. John Cassian, the Roman.

John, too, at an early age, laid aside his books and left the lecture halls to go in search of true wisdom. He went first to the Holy Land and lived there for some years in a monastery in Bethlehem (not that of St. Jerome, though he probably met the saint while there). After a time, his insatiable desire pushed him on. With his abbot's permission and the companionship of one of his brother monks, Herman, he set out to learn still more of the spiritual art and the mystical life from the wise old men hidden in the solitudes and caves of Egypt. It was over seven years before he returned to his monastery, only to seek permission to continue his pursuit. He was never again to return to the Holy Land. In time, he was led from the desert to the capital, ordained a priest, and then sent back to the West, where he established two monasteries near Marseilles— one for women and one for men.

Monasticism was beginning to flourish in fifth-century Gaul, and in response to an expressed need, St. John produced two sets or collections of writings. The first, the *Institutes*, recounted the practices of the monks of Egypt and adapted them for use in the colder, Western regions. Because of the extensive use of the *Institutes* by St. Benedict of Nursia and the tradition he drew upon, Cassian's *Institutes* have had an immense and all-pervading influence on monastic life in the West. In his second collection, St. John included what he considered the most significant teachings he had received in the course of his long pilgrimage. These he presented in the form of *Conferences* given by various great Fathers of the Desert.

As Cassian himself tells us, one day he and Herman visited the famous Abba Isaac and sought from him a teaching on prayer. The saintly old man obliged, and this teaching has come down to us as the very beautiful and deep "First Conference of Abba Isaac on Prayer." That night, John and his companion fairly floated back to their cell, so uplifted were they by the transcendent teaching of this great Father. But when they awoke in the morning, their feet again solidly planted on Mother Earth, Herman turned to his companion with the important question: "Yes, but how do you do it?" And the two young monks ran back across the sands to the cell of the elder to pose this question to him. Abba Isaac's "Second Conference" is his response to this question. In it we find the first written expression in the West of that tradition of prayer of which Centering Prayer is a contemporary presentation.

The whole of Abba Isaac's magnificent Conference should certainly be read. But let us here listen to just a few of the words of this wise old man, the ones that most directly relate to our present concern:

> I think it will be easy to bring you to the heart of true prayer. . . . The man who knows what questions to ask is on the verge of understanding; the man who is beginning to understand what he does not know is not far from knowledge.

> I must give you a formula for contemplation. If you carefully keep this formula before you, and learn to recollect it at all times, it will help you to mount to contemplation of high truth. Everyone who seeks for continual recollection of God uses this formula for meditation, intent upon driving every other sort of thought from his heart. You cannot keep the formula before you unless you are free from all bodily cares.

> The formula was given us by a few of the oldest fathers who remained. They communicated it only to a very few who were athirst for the true way. To maintain an unceasing recollection of God, this formula must be ever before you. The formula is this: "O God, come to my assistance; O Lord, make haste to help me."

> Rightly has this verse been selected from the whole Bible to serve this purpose. It suits every mood and temper of human nature, every temptation, every circumstance. It contains an invocation of

God, an humble confession of faith, a reverent watchfulness, a meditation on human frailty, an act of confidence in God's response, an
assurance of his ever-present support. The man who continually invokes God as his protector is aware that God is ever at hand.

I repeat: each one of us, whatever his condition in the spiritual life,
needs to use this verse.

Perhaps wandering thoughts surge about my soul like boiling water,
and I cannot control them, nor can I offer prayer without its being
interrupted by silly images. I feel so dry that I am incapable of spiritual feelings, and many sighs and groans cannot save me from
dreariness. I must needs say: "O God, come to my assistance; O
Lord, make haste to help me."

The mind should go on grasping this formula until it can cast away
the wealth and multiplicity of other thoughts, and restrict itself to
the poverty of this single word. And so it will attain with ease that
Gospel beatitude which holds first place among the other beatitudes: "Blessed are the poor in spirit, for theirs is the kingdom of
heaven." Thus by God's light the mind mounts to the manifold
knowledge of God, and thereafter feeds on mysteries loftier and
more sacred. . . . And thus it attains that purest of pure prayers to
which our earlier conference led, so far as the Lord deigns to grant
this favor; the prayer which looks for no visual image, uses neither
thoughts nor words; the prayer wherein, like a spark leaping up
from a fire, the mind is rapt upward, and, destitute of the aid of the
senses or of anything visible or material, pours out its prayer to
God. . . .

For the better part of ten centuries, the monastic approach to
prayer prevailed, beginning with the first attempts at written trans-
mission, by such men as Evagrius Ponticus and John Cassian in the
fourth century, until the prevalence of scholastic thinking in the
Western Christian community, which in the fourteenth century
brought about a divorce between theology and spirituality. For the
monk, life was integral. It was all *one*, and in practice he did not
distinguish between reading or study of the Scriptures and prayer,
or between meditation and contemplation. There was just one simple movement of response to a God who had spoken, a God who

speaks not just in the books of the divinely inspired Scriptures but in the whole of creation and in the depths of one's own being.

At this point let me inject an important aside. It concerns a semantic difficulty. In our recent Western tradition, when we have spoken of "meditation," we have been understood to refer to a discursive type of prayer in which we consciously reflected on some facet of life, particularly some point of the Scriptures, and sought by this means to arouse in ourselves affective responses and resolutions to guide our conduct. At the same time, "contemplation" has signified for us that moment when our response to the revealed truth or reality was simply being present to it—having passed beyond thinking to simple presence.

For our brothers and sisters in the Hindu tradition, the terms have almost the exact inverse meaning: contemplation is a discursive exercise, and meditation usually means a nonconceptual approach. Perhaps one of the most significant indications of the failure of the Western Christian churches to bring their life-giving tradition even to their own is the fact that the terminology that prevails today in the West is not that of the Western tradition (except perhaps among religious and priests, and those mostly of earlier training) but, rather, the terminology brought to us in recent years by the wise men coming from the Asiatic countries. So there is a difficulty today when we speak of these matters. That is one of the reasons why I prefer to use the term "Centering Prayer" rather than "meditation" or "contemplation." "Prayer" emphasizes what is the essential and oftentimes distinctive element: that of an interpersonal response, a relationship flowing out of love, with another Person or Persons. However, I think it might at times be advantageous, when presenting this form of prayer in a popular context, such as a college campus, to speak of it as "Christian meditation"—meditation being understood in the prevailing, Eastern sense.

But let us return to our monastic tradition. In this tradition, when the monks wished to speak in a reflective way of their experience, they employed four words: *lectio, meditatio, oratio,* and *contemplatio. Lectio,* or more commonly the fuller expression *lectio divina,* cannot be adequately expressed in the simple translation of the word as "reading." We are in fact speaking of a time when perhaps most of the monks and most of the Christian community could not read. Others, of course, could and did read to their illiterate brothers. The choice source for this *lectio* always was and always will be the Sacred Texts. Oftentimes, a simple Christian who could not read would manage to memorize extensive portions of Scriptures, especially the Gospels and the Psalter, so that he could constantly hear it, now recited, as it were, by his own memory.

But *lectio,* in the fuller sense implied here, means the reception of the revelation, by whatever vehicle it may come—the reception of the Word who is the Truth, the Way, and the Life. It may indeed come by way of one's own reading. St. Basil was strongly insistent that all monks learn to read. For us today, our personal time with the Word of Life, with the Sacred Scriptures, is of primary importance. But we also receive this word through the ministry of others, through their reading, and above all, through the Liturgy of the Word. And others will open it out for us in homilies, in instructions, in simple faith-sharing and everyday lived witness. It can also be presented to us, and in fact it has been presented, in art: pictures, frescoes, sculpture, stained glass. The whole Bible can be found in the windows of the cathedral of Chartres. And there were the wonderful mystery plays.

There is also the larger book of revelation: the whole of the work of the Creator, his wonderful creation. All of it speaks of him and of his love for us. Bernard of Clairvaux was fond of saying (to express it in a rather trite translation) that he found God more in the trees and brooks than in the books. *Lectio,* therefore, is receiving the revelation, by whatever means, to be followed quite naturally by *meditatio.*

Again, with *meditatio*—even apart from the semantic difficulty we spoke of above—we have to be careful that our translation be not a betrayal of the truth. In the early monastic tradition, meditation involved primarily a repetition of the word of revelation, or the word of life one received from his spiritual father or from some other source. The word—and here "word" is not to be taken literally as one single word but may be a whole phrase or sentence—was quietly repeated over and over again, even with the lips. Thus the Psalms speak of one meditating with his lips. In time, the repetition would tend to interiorize and simplify the word, as its meaning was assimilated. For during this repetition the mind was not a vacuum. It received the word more and more, entered into it more and more, assimilated it and appropriated it, until it was formed by the word and its whole being was a response to the word.

The Fathers liked to use the image of the cow or other "clean animals who chew the cud." A cow goes out and fills its stomach with grass or other food. Then it settles down quietly and through the process of regurgitation reworks what it has received, moving its lips in the process. Thus it is able to fully assimilate what it has previously consumed and to transform it into rich, creamy milk—a symbol of love filled with the unction of the Holy Spirit. When the received word passes from the lips into the mind and then down into the heart through constant repetition, it produces in the one praying a loving, faith-filled response.

I like very much a distinction made by John Henry Cardinal Newman that I think is very applicable here: What this *meditatio* does is to change a *notional assent* into a *real assent*. As we receive the words of revelation into our mind, they are just so many notions or ideas, which we accept in faith. We do believe. But as we assimilate them through meditation, our whole being comes to respond to them. We move to a real assent. Our whole being, above all our heart, says: "Yes, this is so. This is the reality."

Next—again quite naturally—we turn to *oratio,* to prayer, to response. When God, the loving Creator and Redeemer, so reveals himself, and we really hear that revelation, that Word of Life, we respond with confident assent, with expressed need, with gratitude, with love. This response is prayer. And it bursts out more and more constantly as the reality of our assent deepens and we more fully perceive the revelation of Creator and creative Love in all that we encounter.

Our response grows. It is constantly nourished by illuminating grace. There are moments and seasons of special light. And it is at these times, which eventually become *all* times, that the Reality becomes so real to us that a word or a movement of the heart can no longer adequately respond to it. Our *whole being* must say "yes." This is *contemplatio*. It is a gift, a gift of the Light who is God. We can only open to it, in our God-given freedom, and express our desire to receive it by fidelity to *lectio, meditatio,* and *oratio—oratio* of the most delicate, open, and receptive type. That is what Centering Prayer is. And that is the method that Abba Isaac taught to the two eager young monks, St. John Cassian and his companion, Herman.

The desert tradition out of which this teaching on prayer of John Cassian, *The Cloud of Unknowing,* and Centering Prayer evolved is the same as that from which the Jesus Prayer issued. However, while Abba Isaac gave St. John a word from the Psalms: "O God, come to my assistance; O Lord, make haste to help me," the Eastern current derived its source from two passages of the New Testament—that of the blind Bartimeus and that of the publican—to form the well-known prayer: "Lord Jesus Christ, Son of the Living God, have mercy on me, a sinner." In time, especially under the long domination of the Moslems, the Eastern Christian tradition was enriched or modified by other influences from the East. Thus today the expression "The Jesus Prayer" is a blanket covering a variety of methods. The most highly developed, psychosomatic expression of the Jesus Prayer, presented by Nesophorus of Jerusalem and St. Gregory of Sinai (who actually learned it in Crete and brought it to the Holy Mountain) in the fourteenth century, and by St. Gregory Palamas in the century following, reproduce even to details the dhikr method of the Sufis of the thirteenth century. The Name used by the Sufis, of course, was Allah, while that used by the Orthodox Christians was the Name of Jesus. This dhikr method in its turn reproduces down to details the nembutsu method of meditation used by Buddhists in the twelfth century. We do not necessarily have to postulate a dependency. It may be that spiritual masters coming out of related cultures evolved similar methods.

Alongside this increasingly complicated method there always continued to be present a very simple and pure practice, especially among the Russians and in the sketes on Mount Athos. We find this most recently with Father Silouan, the humble staretz of the Russian monastery on Mount Athos, who died in 1938, and whose life and works have been made known to the West by his disciple

Archimandrite Sophrony. At the end of his long and busy day as dockmaster, the staretz would retire into his office near the abandoned pier, pull his *skouphos* (monk's hat) down over his eyes and ears, and simply enter into the awesome Presence of God, using the saving Name of *Jesus*. His practice at this point was the same as that of the Centering Prayer, with the Name of Jesus as his prayer word.

Other spiritual fathers developed other variations in passing on the tradition, coupling the use of the Name with the breathing or the heartbeat, adopting certain postures, and otherwise seeking to bring the mind down into the heart.

In the West, the tradition remained quite pure until it was virtually lost at the time of the Reformation with the suppression of the monasteries and the defensive repressions of the Inquisition. Flowing from the word St. John Cassian received from Abba Isaac, it did not center on the Name of Jesus but retained a certain suppleness, so that, as the author of *The Cloud of Unknowing* expressed it, each one practicing the prayer would choose his own prayer word—one that is meaningful to him.

Like the Conferences of Abba Isaac, *The Cloud of Unknowing* is the word of a spiritual father addressed to a particular disciple. In the case of *The Cloud,* both the father and the disciple remain unnamed and unknown. We know only that the disciple was still quite young (twenty-four years old) but had nonetheless enjoyed an ongoing relationship with the father. *The Cloud of Unknowing* presupposes the oral instruction the father has given. It is undoubtedly for this reason that we do not find precise instructions by the father in the way of prayer, as with Abba Isaac. But repeatedly in the text there is allusion to such precise instruction and repetition of fragments of it. By drawing these scattered texts together we can, in a rather complete way, reconstruct the precise method of prayer that the father taught his disciple:

Simply sit relaxed and quiet. —Ch. 44

It is simply a spontaneous desire springing . . . toward God. —Ch. 4

Center all your attention and desire on him and let this be the sole concern of your mind and heart. —Ch. 3

The will needs only a brief fraction of a moment to move toward the object of its desire. —Ch. 4

If you want to gather all your desire into one simple word that the mind can easily retain, choose a short word rather than a long one. . . . But choose one that is meaningful to you. Then fix it in your mind so that it will remain there come what may. . . . —Ch. 7

Be careful in this work and never strain your mind or imagination, for truly you will not succeed in this way. Leave these faculties at peace. —Ch. 4

It is best when this word is wholly interior without a definite thought or actual sound. —Ch. 40

Let this little word represent to you God in all his fullness and nothing less than the fullness of God. Let nothing except God hold sway in your mind and heart. —Ch. 40

No sooner has a person turned toward God in love than through human frailty he finds himself distracted by the remembrance of some created thing or some daily care. But no matter. No harm done; for such a person quickly returns to deep recollection. —Ch. 4

Should some thought go on annoying you, demanding to know what you are doing, answer with this one word alone. If your mind begins to intellectualize over the meaning and connotations of this little word, remind yourself that its value lies in its simplicity. Do this and I assure you these thoughts will vanish. —Ch. 7

You are to concern yourself with no creature whether material or spiritual nor in their situation or doings whether good or ill. To put it briefly, during this work you must abandon them all. . . . —Ch. 5

Anyone familiar with Centering Prayer will quite readily discern all the elements of the method in this instruction of the author of *The Cloud of Unknowing*. There is a difference between the instruction of the latter and that of Abba Isaac, even though at times they use the very same words, as when the author of *The Cloud* reechoes Abba Isaac's image: "It is simply a spontaneous desire springing suddenly toward God like sparks from a fire." The difference reflects a development that had taken place in the West and the dissimilarity of the audiences addressed. The *Abba*, addressing himself to monks, spoke in the context of a full life of prayer: *lectio, meditatio, oratio, contemplatio*, as described above. *Meditatio*, the gentle repetition of a word received from *lectio*, was to be the constant occupation of the monk until the meditation, quite naturally as it were, burst into prayer and transcended into contemplation. The author of *The Cloud of Unknowing* might well have been a monk—he certainly was thoroughly familiar with this monastic tradition—yet there is no clear indication that the disciple was; indeed, indications are to the contrary. In any case, the author speaks in a context in which discursive meditation has taken hold. He is well aware of the value of such meditation, yet he urges his disciple to go beyond it and, at least at times, to engage in the work of contemplation. Something of the integrality of the Desert Father is lacking. In some way life seems to be compartmentalized; there is a time for activity, there is a time for discursive meditation, and a time for going beyond all this into contemplation—with a method offered for use during this latter time slot. The author is accepting the reality of the way life is for his disciple and for the larger audience with whom he shares this work; he speaks to the latter and provides for it. Yet it is evident that he has not abandoned the ideal of a wholly integrated life, for he sees this work of contemplation as the best way for his disciple to move toward reintegrating his life.

The author of *The Cloud*, receiving a way of prayer that had developed in the monastic tradition, with great wisdom, prudence, and discretion passes it on in such a way that it can be readily employed by one who does not find himself in a context of life wherein he can be wholly free to seek constant actual prayer. Thus it is that the method of prayer taught by the author of *The Cloud* and represented in Centering Prayer, while certainly not useless to monks, coming as it does from the fullness of their tradition, is yet suited to the life of lay persons as well as to priests and religious who are taken up with the many cares of the active apostolate. *The Cloud of Unknowing* represents a significant molding of tradition responsive to the signs of the times and the needs of God's people. And so, too, we hope, does Centering Prayer.

III

HANDING ON THE GIFT

Perhaps you have had the experience—in a class or on a retreat—the group sits in a circle, the leader takes a ball of soft, impressionable clay, holds it firmly for a few moments, allowing the clay to receive the impression of his hands, and then passes the ball on to his neighbor. The neighbor repeats the action, until the ball has made its way around the entire circle. When the last participant finally receives the ball, it possesses the imprint of each one in the circle. Each has made his or her contribution. Not even a most sagacious Sherlock Holmes could sort out the englobing patterns and assign to each his or her particular contribution. If no member of the group has been excessively forceful, if no one has dropped the ball, and if the handing on has been careful and concerned, the ball will have retained its original roundness. Nothing of its essential form will have been lost, but its physiognomy will have been enriched by the interesting patterns impressed upon it by the fondling of many hands.

That is what *tradition* is: a handing on, from one generation to the next, from one person to another, from spiritual father or mother to attentive son or daughter. Tradition is derived from the Latin word *traditio* (in its verbal form *tradere* or *trans dare*), meaning to give, to pass along, over, or across the generations. No matter how loving, how careful the transmitter may be in his receiving and his passing on, if he has truly received the gift in a personal way, in a fully human way, an impression has been made upon it, an enriching one, for it is the impress of a human person, an image of God, the most glorious of created beings.

We have seen in the previous chapter the earliest recorded articulations of this way of Christian prayer. This gift of life has been handed on through the ensuing centuries, sixteen or so, till it has come down to us today. In our own time it has been gifted with a new name, Centering Prayer, and a new packaging, the impress of our hands as we pass it on to other, younger eager minds and hearts. They, too, as they receive it, mold it and, we hope, will pass it on in a fruitful and life-giving way.

In this chapter I would like, as it were, to turn our examining glass first on one and then on another of the tracings this gift, this way of prayer, has received as it has been handed on. There is no hope of offering a complete examination, for the course has been long and the tracings are exceedingly rich. As justification for the particular ones I share here, I can only offer personal preferences. These are the ones which, in the course of my reading/listening over the years, have stood out as particularly meaningful or beautiful articulations—the impress of particularly beautiful minds and hearts. I have not separated East from West, for, as I have indicated, the Jesus Prayer in its purest form is but another expression of the same tradition springing from the same source.

One of the most articulate of the Desert Fathers was the former courtier and controversial theologian Evagrius Ponticus. A true spiritual father, he has never been accepted in the East (although his writings were widely read under the name of St. Nilos) because of the Origenist errors in his doctrinal works. In the West he is little known. Yet his deep psychological insight has made his articulation of the wisdom of the desert especially useful and valuable. Evagrius championed pure prayer, seeing it as the "laying aside of all thoughts." Let me cite just a few of his beautiful *Chapters on Prayer* which are especially relevant to our topic:

> 69. Stand guard over your spirit, keeping it free of concepts at the time of prayer so that it may remain in its own deep calm. Thus he who has compassion on the ignorant will come to visit even such an

insignificant person as yourself. That is when you will receive the most glorious gift of prayer.

114. Do not by any means strive to fashion some image or visualize some form at the time of prayer.

117. Let me repeat this saying of mine which I have expressed on other occasions: Happy is the spirit that attains to perfect form-lessness at the time of prayer.

119. Happy is the spirit that becomes free of all matter and is stripped of all at the time of prayer.

120. Happy is the spirit that attains to complete unconsciousness of all sensible experience at the time of prayer.

153. When you give yourself to prayer, rise above every other joy—then you will find true prayer.

St. John Climacus receives his surname from the masterful trea-tise he wrote when he was abbot of the monastery on Mount Sinai: *The Ladder of Divine Ascent*. It was the fruit of almost a half cen-tury of monastic living. He died shortly after completing *The Lad-der*, around 649, two hundred and fifty years after Evagrius died in the neighboring Egyptian desert. On the twenty-eighth step of his *Ladder*, St. John speaks of prayer:

5. Let your prayer be completely simple, for both the publican and the prodigal son were reconciled to God by a single phrase. [Recall that it is the prayer of the publican that provides the text for the Jesus Prayer.]

9. Let there be no studied elegance in the words of your prayers. How often the simple and monotonous lispings of little children make their fathers give in to them.

10. Do not launch out into long discussions that fritter away your mind in efforts for eloquence. One word alone spoken by the publican touched God's mercy. A single word full of faith saved the good thief. Prolixity in prayer often fills the mind with images and distracts it, whereas the use of one single word (*monologia*) draws it into recollection.

19. The beginning of prayer consists in banishing the thoughts that

come to us by the use of a single word (*monologistos*) the very moment they appear.

42. During prayer do not let the senses create any images, so as not to be subject to distractions.

But let us now turn for a moment to the West—to a man who has in fact been truly a spiritual father to me: William of Saint Thierry. Abbot William was Bernard of Clairvaux's closest friend, in some ways his mentor, in many ways his adviser. Through the centuries, he has been lost in the shadow of his great friend, but in our times, thanks to renewed scholarship and William's influence on Gabriel Marcel and the Catholic existentialists, he is coming more into his own. In his wonderful little treatise *On Prayer*, William speaks—or, rather, prays—in his characteristic way:

> Lord Jesus Christ, the Truth and the Life, you said that in the time to come the true worshipers of your Father would be those who worshiped you in spirit and in truth. I beseech you, therefore, to free my soul from idolatry [from image-prayer]. Free her, lest in seeking you she should fall in with your companions [the faculties of imagination and memory, which are in man, as it were, companions to the image of God in him, his free will], and begin to stray after their flocks [images coming from the imagination and memory], during the sacrifice of praise. No, let me rather lie down with you and be fed by you in the noon-day heat of your love. By a certain natural sense derived from her First Cause, the soul dreams, after a fashion, of your Face, in the image of which she was herself created. But either because she has lost or has never acquired the habit of not receiving another image in place of it, she is receptive when, in the time of prayer, many other images offer themselves.
>
> If I envisage for you, my God, any form whatever, or anything that has a form, I make myself an idolater.

Then, turning and speaking to himself, he continues:

> . . . rid yourself of all the usual ideas about locality and place and get a firm hold of this: You have found God in yourself. . . . What

is more certain, more dependable, than this, by which our intention may orient itself and on which our affections may lay hold?

But again, if sometimes in our prayer we clasp the feet of Jesus and, attracted to the human form of him who is one Person with the Son of God, develop a sort of bodily devotion, we do not err. Yet, in so doing, we retard and hinder spiritual prayer. He himself tells us, "It is expedient for you that I go away. If I do not go away, the Paraclete will not come to you."

The full significance of the last phrase is seen in the large role William gives to the Holy Spirit in contemplative prayer. He goes on to speak a bit ironically to those whose prayer consists in asking for things:

If, however, we give way completely to laziness and sloth [the *acedia* so bemoaned by the Desert Fathers], and out of the depth of our ignorance cry to God, as out of a dungeon, and want to be heard even when we are not seeking the blessed Face of him to whom we cry; and if we do not care whether he is angry or appeased when he gives us what we want, as long as we get it—well, one who prays like that must be content with what God gives. He does not know how to ask God for great things, so it is nothing great that he receives.

Before leaving my beloved Father William, let me quote just a few lines from one of his *Meditations* (the third), those deeply personal and profoundly human sharings that he published "to help beginners to learn how to pray":

Where are you, Lord, where are you? And where, Lord, are you not? This much at least I know, and that most certainly, that you, in whom we move and have our being, are in a manner present here with me, and that from that most health-giving presence comes the longing and fainting of my soul for your salvation. I know in truth, I am aware most healthfully, that you are with me. I know, I feel, I worship, and I render thanks. But, if you are with me, why am I not with you? What hinders me? What is the obstacle? What gets in the way? If you are with me, working for my good, why am I not in the same way with you, enjoying you, the supreme God of all?

How does perception come into all this? Of what avail are mental images? Can reason, or rational understanding, effect anything? No. For although reason sends us to you, O God, it cannot of itself attain to you. Neither does that understanding which, as a product of reason, has lower matters for its sphere of exercise, go any farther than does reason itself; it is powerless to attain to you.

But, when and how and as far as the Holy Spirit wills, he controls the believing mind, so that something of what you are may be seen by those who in their prayer and contemplation have passed all that you are not, although they do not see you as you are. Nevertheless, this understanding serves to soothe the loving spirit, for there is clearly nothing in it of that which you are not, and although it is not wholly what you are, it is not different from that Reality.

I like, too, this passage from a contemporary of William's, Julian, a monk of Vezelay. It occurs in the first sermon of a series he wrote in his old age:

I pray that the Word of the Lord may come again today to those who are silent, and that we may hear what the Lord God says to us in our hearts. Let us silence the desires and importunings of the flesh and the vainglorious fantasies of our imagination, so that we can freely hear what the Spirit is saying. Let our ears be attuned to the voice that is heard above the vault of heaven, for the Spirit of Life is always speaking to our souls; as Scripture says, "A voice is heard above the firmament which hangs over our heads." But as long as we fix our attention on other things, we do not hear what the Spirit is saying to us.

In the next century, that great mystical theologian St. Bonaventure wrote this in his treatise *On the Perfection of Life:*

Prayer consists in turning the mind to God. Do you wish to know how to turn your mind toward God? Follow my words. When you pray gather up your whole self, enter with your Beloved into the chamber of your heart, and there remain alone with him, forgetting all exterior concerns; and so rise aloft with all your love and all your mind, your affections, your desires, and devotion. And let not your mind wander away from your prayer, but rise again and again in the fervor of your piety until you enter into the place of the wonderful tabernacle, even the house of God. There your heart will be delighted at the sight of your Beloved, and you will taste and see how good the Lord is, and how great is his goodness.

But let us return to the East and the great hesychasts of the fourteenth century. Although it was especially these Fathers who developed the very complex psychosomatic methods of the Jesus Prayer, they were still in touch with its essential simplicity and gave instruction with regard to it.

Nicephorus, in his *Profitable Discourse on Sobriety*, has his interlocutors say: "We beg you to teach us what the attention of the mind is and how to become worthy to acquire it. For this work is quite unknown to us." And the Father responds with a long and rich instruction that says in part:

In the name of our Lord Jesus Christ, who said: "Without me you can do nothing," and having called upon him to help and assist me, I shall try as far as is in my power to show you what attention is and how, God willing, one can succeed in acquiring it.

Some of the saints have called attention the safe-keeping of the mind; others, the guarding of the heart; yet others, sobriety; yet others, mental silence; and others again by other names. But all these names mean the same thing. Just as one can say of bread: a round, a slice, a piece, so also understand about this. As to what attention is and what its characteristic features are, you shall learn forthwith.

Attention is a sign of sincere repentance. Attention is the appeal of the soul to itself, hatred of the world and ascent toward God. Attention is renunciation of sin and acquisition of virtue. Attention is an undoubting certainty of the remission of sins. Attention is the beginning of contemplation, or rather, its necessary condition; for, through attention God comes close and reveals himself to the mind. Attention is serenity of the mind, or rather, its standing firmly planted and not wandering, through the gift of God's mercy. Attention means cutting off thoughts. It is the abode of remembrance of

God and the treasure-house of the power to endure all that may come.

This greatest of all great things may be gained by many, or even by all, mostly by being taught how. A few men receive this gift from God without being taught, working from inner compulsion and the warmth of their faith. But what is rare is not the rule. Therefore it is necessary to seek a teacher who is not himself in error, to follow his instructions, and so to distinguish, by careful attention, defects and excesses to the right or the left encountered through diabolical suggestion. From his own experience of temptations, the teacher will explain to us what is needful and will show us unerringly that mental path which we can then follow with less hindrance. If there is no such teacher at hand, we must search for one, sparing no effort. But even if, after diligent searching, no teacher is to be found, then, with a contrite spirit, calling upon God with tears and assiduous and humble prayer, do what I shall tell you.

. . . do what I shall tell you and with God's help you will find what you seek. You know that in every person, interior conversation takes place in his breast. For, when our lips are silent, it is within ourselves that we speak and hold discourse with ourselves, pray and sing psalms and other things of this kind. Then, having banished every thought from this inner conversation (you can do it if you wish), give it the following short prayer: "Lord Jesus Christ, Son of God, have mercy on me!" and compel it, in place of all other thoughts, to have only this one constant cry within. If you do this continually, with your whole attention, this practice will in time open for you the way to the heart which I have described. There can be no doubt about this, for we have proved it ourselves by experience.

St. Gregory of Sinai (†1346), a contemporary of Nicephorus, who also wrote extensively on hesychasm, the way of inner silence, has this to say:

Keep your mind free from colors, images and forms; beware of the imagination in prayer—otherwise you may find that you have become a fantasist instead of a hesychast.

St. Nil Sorskii (†1408), who perhaps was responsible, more than anyone else, for keeping this tradition so alive among Russian Christians, said much the same:

> So as not to fall into illusion while practicing inner prayer, do not permit yourself any concepts, images or visions.

Undoubtedly the best known teachers of prayer in the West are St. John of the Cross (†1591) and his spiritual mother, St. Teresa of Ávila (†1582). Unfortunately, the fretful spirit of the times, in the form of the Inquisition, oppressed them. Yet the rich heritage they left us, the soaring poetry of the man and the warm, pulsating, earthy wisdom of the woman, speak powerfully to our times. Our regret, if any, is that there are not enough sons and daughters of these two great mystics fully alive with their spirit and bringing it vitally to the multitude who hunger now for such nourishing spiritual food. Let me just share a bit from St. Teresa's *Interior Castle* and her *Way of Perfection,* and from St. John's commentary on his *Living Flame of Love.* In the course of her discourse on the fifth mansion, St. Teresa goes back to the previous mansion and speaks of the soul's experience when first entering into the Prayer of Quiet:

> . . . the soul is doubtful as to what has really happened until it has had a good deal of experience of it. It wonders if the whole thing was imagination, if it has been asleep, if the favor was a gift of God, or if the devil was transfigured into an angel of light. It retains a thousand misgivings. . . . Agile little lizards will try to slip in, though they can do no harm, especially if we take no notice of them. These are the little thoughts that proceed from the imagination, and from what has been said it will be seen that they are often very troublesome.

In the thirty-first chapter of her *Way of Perfection,* the holy mother gives much practical advice to her daughters who are being drawn into the Prayer of Quiet. I am sure some of those who have studied Teresa's teaching would raise objections if one were to say that the Prayer of Centering is the same as the Saint's Prayer of Quiet. I do not intend to imply that here. But I do believe that the practice of the Prayer of Centering does, in God's mercy, readily open out to a state of prayer such as St. Teresa describes here, and so I feel her very practical advice can readily be applied to the experience we have in Centering Prayer. St. Teresa writes:

> It is well to seek greater solitude so as to make room for the Lord and allow His Majesty to do his own work in us. The most we should do is occasionally, and quite gently, to utter a single word, like a person giving a little puff to a candle when he sees it has almost gone out, so as to make it burn again; though, if it were fully alight, I suppose the only result of blowing would be to put it out. I think the puff should be a gentle one because, if we begin to tax our brains by making long speeches, the will may become active again.
>
> Just so, when the will finds itself in this state of quiet, it must take no more notice of the understanding than it would of a madman, for, if it tries to draw the understanding along with itself, it is bound to grow preoccupied and restless, with the result that this state of prayer will be all effort and no gain and the soul will lose what God has been giving it without any effort of its own. Pay great attention to the following comparison, which the Lord suggested to me when I was in this state of prayer, and which seems to me very appropriate. The soul is like an infant still at its mother's breast; such is the mother's care for it that she gives it its milk without its having to ask for it so much as by moving its lips. That is what happens here. The will simply loves, and no effort needs to be made by the understanding, for it is the Lord's pleasure that, without exercising its thought, the soul should realize that it is in his company, and should merely drink the milk which His Majesty puts into its mouth and enjoy its sweetness. The Lord desires it to know that it is he who is granting it that favor and that in its enjoyment of it he too rejoices. But it is not his will that the soul try to understand how it is enjoying this, or what it is enjoying; it should lose all thought of itself, and he who is at its side will not fail to see what is best for it. If it begins to strive with its mind so that the mind may be apprised of what is happening and is thus induced to share in it, it will be

quite unable to do so and the soul will perforce lose the milk and forego that Divine sustenance.

When the understanding (or, to put it more clearly, the thought) wanders off after the most ridiculous things in the world, the soul should laugh at it and treat it as the silly thing that it is, and remain in her state of quiet. For thoughts will come and go, but the will is mistress and all-powerful, and will recall them without your having to trouble about it. But if you try to drag the understanding back by force, you will lose your power over it, which comes from your taking and receiving that divine sustenance, and neither will nor understanding will gain, but both will be losers. There is a saying that, if we try very hard to grasp all, we lose all; and so, I think, it is here. Experience will show you the truth of this; and I shall not be surprised if those of you who have not had this experience think this is very obscure and unnecessary. But, as I have said, if you have only a little experience of it you will understand and will be able to profit by it, and you will praise the Lord for being pleased to enable me to explain it.

John of the Cross, Teresa's friend and disciple, expressed his mystical experience and teaching in magnificent poetry, but for us lesser ones—and for the fathers of the Inquisition—he reinterpreted it in concise and practical prose. In speaking to the person who is passing from active, discursive meditation to contemplative prayer, St. John urges him to "the practice of loving attentiveness" and offers much practical advice in the course of his commentary on the third stanza of *The Living Flame of Love*. Let me cite just one brief passage. He begins with an analogy:

The more the air is cleansed of vapor, and the quieter and more simple it is, the more the sun illumines and warms it. A person should not bear attachment to anything, neither to the practice of meditation nor to any savor, whether sensory or spiritual, nor to any other apprehensions. He should be very free and annihilated regarding all things, because any thought or discursive reflection or satisfaction upon which he may want to lean would impede and disquiet him, and make noise in the profound silence of his senses and his spirit, which he possesses for the sake of this deep and delicate listening. God speaks to the heart in this solitude, which he mentioned through Osee, in supreme peace and tranquillity, while the soul listens, like David, to what the Lord God speaks to it, for he speaks this peace in this solitude.

When it happens, therefore, that a person is conscious in this manner of being placed in solitude and in the state of listening, he should even forget the practice of loving attentiveness I mentioned, so as to remain free for what the Lord then desires of him. He should make use of that loving awareness only when he does not feel himself placed in this solitude or inner idleness or oblivion or spiritual listening.

A good bit of commentary could be written on these words of the masters, in each case showing how they apply to the practice of Centering Prayer. When we do come to speak of the Centering Prayer method in the next chapter, I will refer back to some of these texts. But for now let us go on to listen to another great Spiritual Father of the Russian school of the nineteenth century, Theophan the Recluse, the archbishop who did so much to popularize some of the Western spiritual writings among the Christians of the East. Theophan was one of the Spiritual Fathers who led the revival of traditional spirituality in Russia and gave very clear and concrete instruction on the Jesus Prayer:

There are two ways: the active way, the practice of ascetic labors; and the contemplative way, the turning of the mind to God. By the first way the soul becomes purified and so receives God; by the second way the God of whom the soul becomes aware himself burns away every impurity and thus comes to dwell in the purified soul. The whole of this second way is summed up in the Jesus Prayer, as St. Gregory of Sinai says: "God is gained either by activity and work, or by the art of invoking the Name of Jesus." He adds that the first way is longer than the second, the second being quicker and more effective. For this reason some of the holy Fathers have given prime importance to the Jesus Prayer among all the different kinds of spiritual exercises.

The practice of prayer is called an "art" and it is a very simple one. Standing with consciousness and attention in the heart, cry out unceasingly: "Lord Jesus Christ, Son of God, have mercy on me," without having in your mind any visual concept or image, believing that the Lord sees you and listens to you.

The various methods described by the Fathers (sitting down, making prostrations, and the other techniques used when performing this prayer) are not suitable for everyone; indeed, without a personal director they are actually dangerous. It is better not to try them. There is just one method which is obligatory for all: *to be still with the attention in the heart*. All other things are beside the point and do not lead to the crux of the matter.

It is most important to realize that prayer is always God-given; otherwise we may confuse the gift of grace with some achievement of our own.

The tradition lives on among the Russian émigrés of this century. Staretz Dorofey of Konevitsa, who lived according to the *Sketic Tradition* of St. Nilos, gave this instruction to one of my friends:

Solitude is the exclusion during prayer of all alien thoughts, even those which seem good to us.

In order to avoid spiritual illusions while praying we should not entertain any pictorial representations in our mind, though they will come even when our mind remains in our heart; that is, when we pray with attention and feeling. True unceasing prayer is a state in which we persevere at all times in the adoration of God. This adoration is free from words and images.

Another contemporary, Father Kallistos of Patmos, whose guest I had the joy of being for some days on that most blessed isle, gave voice to the tradition in these words:

The Jesus Prayer is not a form of meditation on specific incidents in the life of our Lord. Rather, it is a method for controlling thoughts, for concentrating the attention and guarding the mind; more precisely, it is a way of containing the mind within the heart. Under normal conditions, a man's attention is scattered and dispersed over a multiplicity of external objects. In order that he may acquire true prayer of the heart, his mind must be unified. It must be brought from fragmentation to singleness, from plurality to simplicity and nakedness; and so it will be enabled to enter and dwell within the heart. Such is the aim of the Jesus Prayer: "By the memory of Jesus Christ," as Philotheus of Sinai puts it, "gather together your mind that is scattered abroad." That is why the Jesus Prayer must be at once uninterrupted and imageless; only thus can it fulfill effectively this task of unification.

Another current of the Eastern Christian tradition is witnessed to and lived out in the West today by Princess Ileana of Romania. The witness of this mother of seven should speak strongly to those who feel they are too busy to find time for prayer. With great simplicity and womanly warmth, the exiled princess gives very practical instruction in the ways of prayer:

We start by following the precepts and examples frequently given us by our Lord. First, go aside into a quiet place: "Come apart into a desert place, and rest a while" (Mk. 6:31); "Study to be quiet" (1 Th. 4:11); then pray in secret—alone and in silence.

The phrases "pray in secret—alone and in silence" need, I feel, a little expanding. "Secret" should be understood as it is used in the Bible: for instance, Jesus tells us to do our charity secretly—not letting the left hand know what the right one does. We should not parade our devotions nor boast about them. "Alone" means to separate ourselves from our immediate surroundings and disturbing influences. As a matter of fact, never are we in so much company as when we pray ". . . seeing we also are compassed about with so great a cloud of witnesses . . ." (Heb. 12:1). The witnesses are all those who pray: angels, archangels, saints and sinners, the living and the dead. It is in prayer, especially the Jesus Prayer, that we become keenly aware of belonging to the living body of Christ. In "silence" implies that we do not speak our prayer audibly. We do not even meditate on the words; we use them only to reach beyond them to the essence itself.

In our busy lives this is not easy, yet it can be done—we can each of us find a few minutes in which to use a Prayer consisting of only a few words, or even only one. This Prayer should be repeated quietly, unhurriedly, thoughtfully. Each thought should be concentrated on Jesus, forgetting all else, both joys and sorrows. Any stray thought, however good or pious, can become an obstacle.

When you embrace a dear one you do not stop to meditate how and why you love—you just love wholeheartedly. It is the same when spiritually we grasp Jesus the Christ to our hearts. If we pay heed to the depth and quality of our love, it means that we are preoccupied with our own reactions rather than giving ourselves unreservedly to Jesus—holding nothing back. Think the Prayer as you breathe in and out; calm both mind and body, using as rhythm the heartbeat. Do not search for words, but go on repeating the Prayer, or Jesus' name alone, in love and adoration. That is ALL! Strange—in this little there is more than all!

But let us now return to the West, using that great teacher of prayer of our times, the Russian Exarch in the West, Archbishop Anthony Bloom, as our bridge person. In his beautiful little book *Beginning to Pray,* he draws on an anecdote belonging to the Western tradition and then gives his own teaching:

In the life of the Curé of Ars, Jean Marie Vianney, there is a story of an old peasant who used to spend hours and hours sitting in the chapel motionless, doing nothing. The priest said to him, "What are you doing all these hours?" The old peasant answered, "I look at him, he looks at me, and we are happy."

This can be reached only if we learn a certain amount of silence. Begin with the silence of the lips, with the silence of the emotions, the silence of the mind, the silence of the body. But it would be a mistake to imagine that we can start at the highest end, with the silence of the heart and the mind. We must start by silencing our lips, by silencing our body in the sense of learning to keep still, to let tenseness go, not to fall into daydreaming and slackness, but, to use the formula of one of our Russian saints, to be like a violin string, wound in such a way that it can give the right note, neither wound too much to the breaking point, nor too little so that it only buzzes. And from then onward we must learn to listen to silence, to be absolutely quiet, and we may, more often than we imagine, discover that the words of the Book of Revelation come true: "I stand at the door and knock."

Father George Maloney, S.J., a Western spiritual father, who has entered deeply into the Eastern tradition, has sought to bring its life-giving currents to the West. His teaching on the Prayer of the Heart, or Centering Prayer, is, then, no different. Note these few sentences from his book *Inward Stillness:*

> To enter into God's dance of exuberant joy and fullness of life we must descend. This descent is a descent into the deepest reaches of our consciousness and our unconscious. It is really an ascent to God who dwells in the secret recesses of our hearts. It is simply growing into greater, expanded consciousness through prayer.

> To pray to the Father in the inner sanctuary of our heart, with the clearest, purest consciousness of his abiding love, and our sincere desire to surrender totally to him by a reformed life of love towards others, we must get rid of any dispersion of inner attention. Love does not grow when we are scattered about in our thoughts, but rather when we are deeply focused and concentrated on the one we love.

Hans Urs von Balthasar expresses this thought more tersely:

> Contemplation is an inward gaze into the depths of the soul and, for that very reason, beyond the soul to God.

And that thought very directly and immediately brings us to the great spiritual master of the West in our century, from whom Centering Prayer has derived its name, Father Louis of Gethsemani, better known as Thomas Merton:

> . . . prayer begins not so much with "consideration" as with a "return to the heart," finding one's deepest center, awakening the profound depths of our being in the presence of God who is the source of our being and of our life.

I have already quoted some of the most pertinent passages from

Father Louis's writings relative to Centering Prayer in *Daily We Touch Him*. There are many, many more I could quote. But here I would like to quote just a few of the *novissima verba*—the last words of this wonderful spiritual father. On the eve of his historic flight to the Orient, Father spent a couple of days with the Cistercian nuns at Redwoods Abbey, in California. In the course of his sharing there with the special friends who had gathered from many corners, he said many very beautiful things. Here are some of the most pertinent to our concern:

> The great thing is prayer. Prayer itself. If you want a life of prayer, the way to get it is by praying. We were indoctrinated so much into means and ends that we don't realize that there is a different dimension in the life of prayer. In technology you have this horizontal progress, where you must start at one point and move to another and then another. But that is not the way to build a life of prayer. In prayer we discover what we already have. You start where you are and you deepen what you already have. And you realize that you are already there. We already have everything, but we don't know it and we don't experience it. Everything has been given to us in Christ. All we need is to experience what we already possess. The trouble is we aren't taking time to do so.

> If we really want prayer, we'll have to give it time. We must slow down to a human tempo and we'll begin to have time to listen. And as soon as we listen to what's going on, things will begin to take shape by themselves.

> This is what the Zen people do. They give a great deal of time to doing whatever they need to do. That's what we have to learn when it comes to prayer. We have to give it time.

> What truly matters is not how to get the most out of life, but how to recollect yourself so that you can fully give yourself.

> What is keeping us back from living lives of prayer? Perhaps we don't really want to pray. This is the thing we have to face. Before this we took it for granted that we were totally dedicated to this desire for prayer. Somebody else was stopping us.

> It is a risky thing to pray, and the danger is that our very prayers

get between God and us. The great thing in prayer is not to pray, but to go directly to God. If saying your prayers is an obstacle to prayer, cut it out. Let Jesus pray. Thank God Jesus is praying. Forget yourself. Enter into the prayer of Jesus. Let him pray in you.

The best way to pray is: stop. Let prayer pray within you, whether you know it or not. This means a deep awareness of your true inner identity.

By grace we are Christ. Our relationship with God is that of Christ to the Father in the Holy Spirit.

There are no levels. Any moment you can break through into the underlying unity which is God's gift in Christ. In this end, Praise praises. Thanksgiving gives thanks. Jesus prays. Openness is all.

A contemporary American, one who is effectively handing on the tradition today, develops the idea of our identity with Jesus in prayer and ties it in with the full meaning of the prayer word. In a delightful yet profound article, *The Man Who Was the Lord's Prayer*, Father Ed Hays writes:

To learn how to pray is not to learn new poetic words. To learn how to pray is to learn how to pronounce your own sacred word —go speak yourself! To learn to pray is not to learn some method. It is to know who you are and to be who you are supposed to be!

You are prayer. You are a special and sacred word of God made flesh. To pronounce your own unique word is to pray the most beautiful—if not the holiest—of prayers. Jesus was a prayerful man, not because he prayed prayers (which he did), but because he *was* prayer! Jesus was true to the Word that came from his Father, the Word that was himself. In being who he was supposed to be, he found a cure for the ancient sickness of aphasia. That cure lies in speech therapy and in being true to his Word and to your word. Remember that he said, "Anyone who loves me will be true to my Word."

Thus through the centuries, again and again, spiritual fathers and mothers repeat, each in his or her own spirit-filled way, the same saving message: We are prayer, we are the Son to the Father, we have received the Spirit, we need but be silent and be who we are, and let Prayer, the Spirit of All Prayer, pray within us.

This is our heritage, the tradition, and in receiving the gift of Centering Prayer, we enter deeply into it, let it become truly ours, a part of us, and receive the responsibility ourselves to pass it on. In this regard I would like to close this chapter with some words from one of the great living fathers of the Church, Father Henri de Lubac, S.J.:

> Being a man of the Church, he will love her past. He will meditate over her history, holding her tradition in veneration and exploring deep into it. He will take pleasure in going back in spirit to the age of the new-born Church when, as St. Irenaeus put it, the echo of the Apostles' preaching was still audible, "Christ's blood still warm and faith burned with a living flame in the heart of the believer." But her tradition for him is no more a thing of the past than of the present, but rather a great living and permanent force which cannot be divided into bits and pieces, for he believes both that God revealed to us in His Son all that is to be revealed, once and for all, and that the Church, saying nothing on her own account, merely follows and declares this divine revelation, guided by the Holy Spirit who is given to her as her teacher.
>
> What the man of the Church will look for is not so much the company of great intellectuals as that of truly spiritual men, and he will, as far as possible, be on intimate terms with those who prayed to Christ and who lived, worked, thought, and suffered for him in the Church before him; for such men are fathers of his soul.
>
> He will see that many non-essential things change according to time and place, but this will not blind him from making it his business to see the continuity which exists at an even deeper level of reality. And though excluding nothing from his view, his personal preferences will be for the age of the first martyrs, the rise of monasticism, the main stage in the formation of dogma, the work of the great saints and doctors; and far from taking pleasure in this, much as one who tours the monuments of a great city, he will do so so as to be wholly at the service of the great community, sharing its happiness and its trials and developing a sensibility ever more alive to

the cause of Christ. For such a man could never be an idle spectator when he knows that Christ is always present, today as yesterday and right up to the consummation of the world, and that the Church, with the very bonds with which she seems to bind us, has no other aim than that of freeing us, uniting us and giving us room to live and breathe the very life of Christ.

Centering Prayer, coming out of the tradition, is a way today "of freeing us, uniting us and giving us room to live and breathe the very life of Christ."

IV

A NEW PACKAGING

Two things are new about Centering Prayer: the name and the packaging. Old wine in new wineskins—which is good—not new wine in old wineskins, which is often a problem in our Christian communities today. People in marketing tell us the way to sell an old product is to give it a new name and an attractive wrapper and off you go! Actually, "selling it" was not at all the intent in the development of Centering Prayer. The new name came to be almost by accident and caught on quite readily. The new packaging was devised to respond to a very real need.

There is no copyright on the name "Centering Prayer." Others were using it before it began to be applied to this particular method of prayer. And it is still being used in a general sense to refer to any method by which the pray-er seeks to bring his or her scattered thoughts and feelings together to allow for a certain deepening.

The name came to be applied to this particular method in the course of the first workshop I was sharing with a group of religious superiors under the auspices of the Conference of Major Superiors of Men. (The participants were actually divided equally among men and women.) Prior to that workshop we had been speaking of "the prayer of *The Cloud*"—referring to *The Cloud of Unknowing*, the primary written source we were employing—or simply "a method of contemplative prayer."

In the course of that workshop, I referred frequently to Thomas Merton, whom I had the privilege of knowing personally and whom I consider one of the great spiritual fathers of our times. In his writings Tom spoke frequently of attaining to the experience of God by going to one's center and passing through it into the center of God. For example, in the last book that he himself prepared for publication (which was still in galleys when he died), *The Climate of Monastic Prayer*, he wrote:

> Monastic prayer begins not so much with "considerations" as with a "return to the heart," finding one's deepest center, awakening the profound depths of our being in the presence of God, who is the source of our being and of our life.

Although Centering Prayer is an extremely simple and pure method of prayer, it is not yet wholly free from some use of symbols, at least not until it opens out into the transcendent experience. This may take place almost immediately, but still in the first moments, as we move into the Prayer, we use some thought, affection, and image. During the progress of the prayer, we seek to employ—only to the extent truly necessary—the subtlest and most human of symbols, a very simple word. As the author of *The Cloud* says: "A one-syllable word such as 'God' or 'love' is best." But in moving into the Prayer, most find the rather subtle imaginative symbol of the "center" very effective. This place—which we make no attempt at pinpointing physically or imaginatively—is deep within, deep within our spirit. It is the place of encounter with the living Triune God. It is the place where at every moment we come forth into being by his loving creative action. It is the "ground of our being," to use another Merton simile.

The name "Centering Prayer" well expresses the effective imaginative activity that is present in the initial movement of faith and love that brings us to Presence. And because it is a good name, it has stuck and has become the common and popular name for this particular method of entering into contemplative prayer or deep meditation, drawn from our Western Christian tradition and taught by the author of *The Cloud of Unknowing*.

Merton thought highly of *The Cloud of Unknowing*. In the introduction to Father William Johnston's book *The Mysticism of the Cloud of Unknowing*, he wrote: "Indeed there has never been a book on mysticism that showed such realistic common sense as *The Cloud*." The famous Benedictine spiritual writer Father Baker said its mysticism is "ordinary." And Johnston himself rightly points out that such mysticism is "no more than an intensification of the ordinary Christian life."

The symbol of the "cloud" has a biblical basis. Christ is the Way, the Truth, and the Life. It is by following him—the Way—that we come to Truth and Life. But the day came when his disciples followed him up a hill—in Galilee or Olivet near Jerusalem or wherever, we are not quite sure—and he rose up from their midst and entered into a cloud. And their eyes and their hearts followed him. Thenceforth he was to be found only in the cloud of faith. He had told them: "It is expedient for you that I go away." And his ardent, late-born apostle reminded the faithful: "Once we knew him in the flesh, but we know him so no longer."

Yet, for most of us, the analogy of the cloud is not the most meaningful or effective one. Few of us have been in a cloud, except perhaps when we have been enclosed in that space capsule we call an airplane. I remember well my first experience of being in a cloud. It was on the occasion of my first visit to Europe. When we landed in Barcelona, the superintendent of the steamship line was kind enough to arrange for someone to drive me up to the Abbey of Montserrat. Just outside the city of Barcelona there leaps up out of the plains a soaring mass of granite that reaches to the clouds. For forty-five minutes our car wound round and round this mass, climbing ever higher, till at length we reached the immense monastery that is perched near the top.

My visit there was a wonderful experience. I arrived in time for what was, by Spanish standards, a latish supper—11 P.M. In the morning I was treated to the Mass of the Trinity sung at dawn by the boy oblates, and then to the community Mass, at which some fourteen thousand pilgrims from the seventeen provinces of Spain, each in their particular traditional garb, joined the monks and boys in praising God. Then there was a fiesta in the square. After lunch I took a walk up the road with some of the boy oblates. Below us—every detail of it brought out by the brilliant noonday sun—was the fascinating, ancient, and in many ways charming port city of Barcelona. The busy harbor, the sea, the coastal plains stretching north and south—it was magnificent. Suddenly a low cloud came along. We were enveloped. I could see virtually nothing. The whole vast panorama I had been enjoying a moment before was gone. I could hardly perceive the lads around me. I was in a cloud of unknowing. The sudden quiet, the coolness, invited one to go within. Yet there was a certain fearfulness, an impulsive need to push through to the reality I knew was about me. I found myself "beating against the cloud," and realized what an effortless beating it was. With such an experience, the analogies of our unknown English author made a great deal of sense to me. Without such an experience, one is apt to miss much of their meaning.

But even having had such an experience, I think I prefer the analogy of the center. It evokes less imagination. It is almost an imageless image. And it is something that is always with us—who can be without a center? It is perhaps akin to the empty circle that is used to represent Zen.

The Christian East prefers to use the more specifically human and sensible image of the heart—the Prayer of the Heart. This accords well with the centrality of love in this work of contemplation. But the heart, through our scientific studies, has been made so anatomically physical and, through our secular popularizations and through some popular devotions, so sentimental, that it does not serve well for Westerners.

I think, all in all, the image of the center serves best for most of us.

The new packaging is the formulation of the method in three rules. The formulation found in *Daily We Touch Him* and *Finding Grace at the Center* (see Bibliography) represents an initial endeavor and was meant to be tentative, subject to refinement according to the dictates of a widening experience. At this point it could perhaps stand a bit of refurbishing or at least a more nuanced interpretation. But, as a starting point, let us repeat the three rules here:

Rule One: At the beginning of the Prayer we take a minute or two to quiet down and then move in faith to God dwelling in our depths; and at the end of the Prayer we take several minutes to come out, mentally praying the "Our Father" or some other prayer.

Rule Two: After resting for a bit in the center in faith-full love, we take up a single, simple word that expresses this response and begin to let it repeat itself within.

Rule Three: Whenever in the course of the Prayer we become *aware* of anything else, we simply gently return to the Presence by the use of the prayer word.

There are some who prefer to divide the first rule, considering the second phrase of it as a fourth rule, thus following the chronological sequence of the experience. With all reverence for the strong tradition that calls for all good things to come in threes, such a fourfold presentation certainly has its merits.

Others like to prefix a rule or two for relaxing or add some method such as a countdown or breath-watching to aid the quieting and moving into the depths. I would like to counsel against this. I think that in practice very many, if not most, do in actual fact add some routine they follow and find helpful when coming to Centering Prayer. I certainly have no objection to this. Everywhere and always the wise words of old Dom Chapman hold: "Pray as you can, don't pray as you can't." We use a method only to facilitate, to assist. The purer and simpler we keep the method, the more apt it is to assist us to find purity and simplicity in our prayer, and the less apt it is to become burdensome and distracting baggage. Above all, when we are teaching others, we should pass on the teaching in all purity and not make the accidentals we have found personally helpful a rule for others. Let them find their own helps under the guidance of the Spirit. We might share, as suggestive, things we have found helpful, but let us not make them into rules or hand them on as part of the tradition.

We are indeed very prone to complexify things, and we have to be watchful of this. The prayer in itself is very simple. We just let go and let God do. It doesn't leave much room for us to take pride

or credit, or claim a reward. We find that hard. We like complicated things. We can pat ourselves on the back for being so smart as
to understand and master them. We need to hold on to those words
of the author of *The Cloud:* ". . . remind yourself that its value lies
in its simplicity." "Unless you become as a little one, you will not
enter into the kingdom."

I do not mean by this to discourage anyone from taking some
time and indeed using some routine or method for relaxing and
quieting down before entering into the Prayer. I will, in fact, in a
later chapter suggest some simple methods for relaxing. If one can
simply sit down and immediately be relaxed and enter into the
Prayer, that's good; if one regularly uses a little relaxation exercise,
that's good too. But we should not make that exercise a part of the
Centering Prayer method as such, especially when we are teaching others. It is very important to relax before entering into
the Prayer and even to take a little bit of time to do so. It is important, so that the body can be refreshed in the Prayer; it is important
also so that the body, letting go and resting in the chair, can be a
sacrament of what we seek to do in the spirit: let go and rest in
God.

I do not think it is too gross an oversimplification to say that
there are essentially two kinds of prayer or meditation: the effortful
and the effortless. Zen, especially of the Rinsi school, is effortful.
The meditator adopts a very rigid posture, one that calls the whole
being to a certain keenness of attention. The eyes are kept partially
open. The meditator is goaded on with the stick. The mind works
relentlessly with its enigmatic koan. Finally there is the break-
through. The chick pierces the shell. The Risen Lord bursts from
the tomb. The meditator enters into the universal compassion of the
cosmic Christ.

The discursive meditation of many of the later Christian methods
is of this effortful sort. The meditator works with intellect and
affections until suddenly the truth breaks open and reveals itself in
all its wonder, and then he or she can be present to it in contemplative awe and adoring love.

TM and the mantric type of prayer taught by Father John Main
(see Bibliography) are of the effortless type. One simply lets go,

employing as gently as possible the assonance of a specially chosen sound-word to facilitate the letting go, ever ready to let the mantra itself go.

Centering Prayer also is of the effortless type. That is why it is important to relax, to find the place, the posture, the chair that facilitate this, and gently to close the eyes, for it is estimated that twenty-five percent of our psychic energy is expended in seeing.

We cannot always find the ideal place. We might well find ourselves meditating on the morning express or in an air terminal or above a busy, noisy city street. So be it. We can still meditate. And the important thing is to meditate. But obviously, if we can find a place where we are less battered by sounds and the vibrations of frenetic energies, our system will have less to cope with during the meditation. We will probably have a more peaceful meditation and be more rested at the end.

We in the West are not so sensitively aware of vibrations. Yet they inevitably take their toll on us. A room that has been very full of busy activity or loud, hard music carries its charge long after. It is well to be aware of this when we have a choice of places to meditate. When Father Silouan went down in the evening to pray in his office on the abandoned pier, although all seemed quiet he would still pull his hat down over his eyes and ears to free himself even more from the remains of the day's activities.

A particular place can certainly become a supportive context. An icon or the Sacred Text can be a sanctifying presence there. Associations can build up. Previous meditations can leave their mark. And so, in so far as it might be possible, it is good to have our meditation room or corner, to which we will regularly repair. But, again, meditation itself is the important thing, and we can really do it any place, any time. A friend recently shared with me how in the midst of a wedding reception he and a few others slipped off to a corner to meditate.

Time, too, is a consideration. Some times are indeed better than others. Tradition has always pointed to the early hours of the morning. We are naturally quiet after the night's rest, and all creation is in quietness. Everything conspires to facilitate our entering into the silence. "Be still," it all seems to say, "and know that he is God."

Shortly after rising and freshing up, before energizing ourselves
with food or strenuous exercise, is the best time for most, though
some find jogging or other exercise a good preparation.

The late afternoon is, again, a traditional time for prayer—
Vespers. The day is tiring, quieting, and so are we, though there
may yet be many hours of evening activity ahead. Before the evening jog, or perhaps after it, but certainly before the meal, is a good
time to take twenty minutes to sit quietly with the Lord and be
deeply refreshed and renewed.

No time is really ruled out. Waking in the night, we might turn
to centering. Some find it an excellent way to prepare for sleep,
though others have found it might so renew them that they will
have difficulty getting a full night's sleep. After meals is perhaps
the poorest time, for our center is elsewhere, our metabolism is way
up; yet it is better than no time at all.

We have encouraged twenty-minute meditations. Most find this a
good pace. Some find themselves settling for a little less or a little
more. Religious and others who recognize prayer as a major part of
their particular vocation and service usually opt for longer periods.
But shorter periods are not to be ruled out. Ten minutes is better
than five, and five better than none, though we might want to reex-
amine our priorities if that seems to be all we are able to allow ourselves for something that so touches the center of our being and
life. Along with our two basic meditations, we may well find our
rhythm opening out into a third, perhaps shorter one, at midday, or
even many quite short ones as we move along through the day from
one area of activity to another or from one engagement to another.
The prayer word itself may at times come on its own to summon us
to what my brother calls a "quickie." As the author of *The Cloud*
reminds us, time "needs only a brief fraction of a moment" to move
into eternity.

Much could be said about posture, too. Apart from malformation,
disability, or the effects of some special training, the human body
pretty much works the same for all. That means it is most natural,
most comfortable, most open to relaxation and refreshment when
the back is essentially straight. Illness or exhaustion may leave us in
a prone position. This does not rule out meditating. On the con-

trary, in such a state we can greatly profit from meditation. The postures coming from the East are not counterindicated either, for those who can well employ them. But, for most of us in the West, a good chair that well supports the back offers the best opportunity for finding the right posture for Centering Prayer.

Place, time, posture are important, for we are incarnational people, and all is sacramental of the Presence of Creative Love. But prayer goes beyond sign and sacrament. They can be supportive and helpful. But we can pray without them. The spirit is ultimately free.

Let us now turn to the three or four rules.

The question that is asked most frequently in regard to the first rule is: "Just what is meant when we say we are 'to move in faith to God dwelling in our depths'?" We are, of course, using spatial images here to try to express a purely spiritual act. God, in fact, dwells in no place, and yet he is in every place. We can find him equally in the heights or in the depths, within or without, wherever we will. So we could just as easily say simply, ". . . move in faith to God." But most of us do find it initially helpful to sort of locate God in a place, sense him there, as it were; and a good place for this, if we are trying to collect and focus ourselves, is deep within, in the center of our being.

But, then, what kind of motion is faith? How do we move in faith? The motion of faith is really *love*. Revelation tells us of God's presence. In faith we assent to this reality. Enlightened by faith, moved by God's grace, we say: "Yes, God is present." Our faith tells us too that God deserves our attention; he is the source of all our good, of all that we are, of all that is. He is the most loving, the most benevolent; he is our Father, our Brother, our Savior, our Friend beyond all friends. The perception of such a good one, of such a friend, invokes that response we call love: an appreciation of who he is, a desire to be with him, to be one with him, to be united with him, to acknowledge his wonderfulness, his goodness; to praise him, to thank him, to embrace him—just simply to be totally *to him*. This is to move in living faith.

The Prayer, then, begins with those elements we have spoken of in an earlier chapter: the *lectio*, or reception in what is hardly more

than an instantaneous recall of the goodness of God's personal creative and redeeming love, the *meditatio*, or momentary reflection on
this, evoking the *oratio*, or response of faith-full love, the movement
of faith, which brings us into the Presence, and then we are ready
for the *contemplatio*, to simply *be* to that wonderful Presence. It is
simple, it is full, it is total.

In a fraction of a minute—and ordinarily we should not take
much more than that—we pass into a prayer of quiet recollection, of
presence. And it is there we wish to stay, in a state of loving attention. To facilitate this we have the second rule, which is perhaps
the most subtle aspect of this method: the presence and the use of
the prayer word, the word of love.

In the first place, beginners often sense a great concern about just
what word to use. This is perhaps because of the emphasis in some
Eastern methods on having the right mantra. Or it may just flow
out of our rather habitual need to be right, and to be sure we are
right and are doing things the right way. In actual fact, we can almost say it doesn't matter what word we use, or if we even use a
sound that is not an intelligible word in any language we know, but
to which we have given meaning in this instance.

The author of *The Cloud of Unknowing* does say, ". . . choose
one that is meaningful to you." That is the important thing: that the
word or sound we use has meaning for us—and that meaning is
love. It is a love word, or to put it another way, it sums up in a few
letters, in a single syllable, that movement of faith-full love with
which we have begun our prayer. The word abides as a present
sacrament, a perduring prolongation of the initial movement.

I do not want to deny the value that the sound quality of a word
might have to facilitate inner quiet and meditation. We in the West
with our ever-increasing noise pollution are perhaps all too insensi-
tive to the effect that vibrations of all kinds, and especially sound
vibrations, can and do have on us. The mantras used in certain
Hindu traditions for meditation are chosen precisely in view of
their sound quality. Their effectiveness has led sometimes to certain
divine qualities being attributed to them in later, more popular
religion. There is no doubt that certain sounds do have a quieting
effect. And I think when we choose our prayer word, our word of

love, we quite instinctively choose a quieting word, a gentle word, a soft word that quiets the mind and allows the heart space.

For most people, the prayer word is a vocative word. When we truly love someone, we have a name for him or her. It may be a proper name or it may be a pet or nickname. And when we speak that name it expresses our whole relation to that person. It may be Mom, or Mama, or Mother, or Madre; whatever it be, it expresses our whole relation to that very special woman in our lives, and no other word quite does it. My mother always called her father *Papa*. But if I called my dad *Papa*, I think we would have both felt a bit awkward, to say the least.

If we have a real relation going with God, then we have a name for him that quite spontaneously comes to mind when we turn our attention to him. And that is, oftentimes, the word that best serves us as our prayer word. It is not infrequent that for a Christian the prayer word is the holy Name *Jesus*. And it is then, when the prayer word is Jesus, that the two great traditions, springing from the one source, reunite. Centering Prayer and the Jesus Prayer are once again one, as they were long ago in the hearts of the Fathers of the Desert.

The prayer word, then, might well be a name or a vocative word; yet it need not necessarily be. I know a very beautiful sister for whom the prayer word is "let go." That expresses the whole essence of her relation with her Divine Beloved. It is true that such a prayer word is more than one syllable, it is more than one word. And such a sentence might well lead to a certain amount of intellectual or conceptual activity. We have to take care. As the author of *The Cloud* has said: "If your mind begins to intellectualize over the meaning and connotations of this little word, remind yourself that its value lies in its simplicity." We can be quite free in choosing a prayer word that is meaningful to us.

Here is perhaps something of the difference between Eastern techniques and Christian prayer. "Where the Spirit is, there is freedom." The typical Eastern technique, seeking to achieve something in itself by the very activity of the one performing it, demands absolute fidelity to the technique until the end is attained. For the Christian, prayer is always a response. God initiates the activity and indeed is the source of our response. We, the pray-ers, move with the Spirit of God. "We do not know how to pray as we ought, but the Spirit prays within us. . . ." We are human. We are incarnate. We can and do use methods. But we can use them with the greatest of freedom. And the use of a prayer word is a method most suitable for us as Christians. God has spoken to us. We have received the Revelation. We have received the Word. If God speaks his love to us most totally and eloquently in a human Word that is divine, we can most aptly respond in a human word that is divinized by faith and love in the action of the Holy Spirit.

The mantric type of prayer taught by Father John Main, while retaining this essential Christian note, and in this way appealing to the same, Cassian tradition, yet approaches more closely the Eastern techniques. Indeed, in his writings and talks Father freely acknowledges his dependence on the experience he had at the feet of a Hindu master during his service in the East—an experience that was brought to fullness when he became a Benedictine and came into contact with the teaching of St. John Cassian. Thus, instead of having the meditator choose his or her own meaningful prayer word, Father encourages each to use the word *Maranatha,* a word chosen for its assonance and because for most Christians it does not have strong conceptual connotations. And this word is to be repeated constantly during the time of prayer. Father concludes his remarks in one article:

> As to frequency, you must say the mantra for the entire time of your meditation to the rhythm you find for yourself. You will be tempted to rest on your oars. . . . The way to transcend the temptation is absolute fidelity to the mantra. This is the condition of rooting it in your heart.

This approach is quite different from that of Centering Prayer. And this brings us to the third rule:

> Whenever in the course of the Prayer we become aware of anything else we simply gently return to the Presence by the use of the prayer word.

We do not use the prayer word constantly. It sort of hovers in our mind, somewhat like white sound. In an office or library or bank, we sometimes find quiet background music. It is not there for people to stop and listen to it. Rather, it is there to block out or blur other sounds so we can be more free to attend to our errand. And so the prayer word, recalled at the beginning of our meditation, lies quietly in our consciousness, leaving us free simply to attend to the Lord of our love. We do not make any effort to repeat the prayer word. We certainly do not turn it into an affective ejaculation. Nor do we make an effort not to repeat the word. We certainly do not judge the perfection of our prayer either by the frequency or infrequency with which we use the word. We do not make it the aim of our prayer to decrease the frequency with which we use the word. We simply seek to be wholly present in love to God present to us, and whenever something draws us away from that Presence, we very gently employ the word to return fully to the Holy Presence.

We may indeed find that some days we seem to have to use the word constantly. No matter. This should cause us no distress. We just repeat the prayer word as gently as possible. To begin to get distressed, or to try to use the word forcefully to eliminate thoughts will only take us more out of the Prayer. The gentle repetition of the word will, on the other hand, place us ever more deeply and totally in the Prayer, the movement into God that goes on underneath the thoughts and surface activity.

I think we all, at times, flirt with the rather presumptuous thought that if we had been God we could have done a better job of it, setting up this world and making it run right. If I had been creating the human person, I would surely have improved on the model. I would have put into us some turn-off switches so that when we wanted to meditate we could simply turn off the thoughts, turn off the imagination, turn off the hearing, turn off the feelings. Ah, then, what peaceful meditations we would have! But God did not provide us with such fine equipment—and for his own very good reasons.

There is a very good analogy that comes from the great Saint Teresa. When she was an old woman—very much a woman of prayer, and a very busy woman, hurrying about Spain reforming the men as only a woman can—she said in effect that she experienced her life as if it were two rivers: one river was constantly flowing into God; the other, into all those business affairs. And yet the two rivers were one river.

I like this analogy very much. Our lives are great flowing rivers, full of vitality and force. And because we are men and women who believe and who love God, the rivers of our lives are flowing powerfully into God at all times. That is the deep current of our lives. But on the surface we have all sorts of things scurrying about: heavily laden freighters, pleasure yachts, busy little tugs, whizzing hovercrafts, garbage scows, and our own collection of pollution and debris. We've got it all! And it all flows right along with us.

In Centering Prayer we sink down into the quiet depths, where there is only a simple, peaceful flow from our Source into the Ocean of Infinite Love. What serenity, what tranquillity, what peace; what vitality, what power, what refreshment! But, on the surface, a lot of activity is still going on. Thoughts are still careening along, feelings are being evoked, sounds are hitting our eardrums. And every once in a while, a flashy vessel or a particularly interesting one arrests our attention and we find ourselves surfacing —or perhaps we have fully surfaced and all but climbed aboard the enticing boat before we are *aware* of having left the peaceful depths.

It is at this point that we use our prayer word. We do not so much turn from the thought or feeling. We do not think (another thought) of letting it go. We simply—with the gentlest repetition of our prayer word, maybe only the faintest recollection of it—return to the Presence. The author of *The Cloud* says, "It is best when this word is wholly interior, without a definite thought or actual sound." We simply, peacefully sink again into the depths. It is as gentle and effortless as that: a sinking down into the depths. If we but let ourselves go, we have a natural propensity to rest quietly in our Source. And so, throughout our prayer time, the thoughts, the feelings, the sounds, the images continue. We just let them flow along. Our attention is elsewhere.

To use another analogy that might be more familiar to some: Suppose we are at a cocktail party. The room is crowded. Standing in little groups, glasses in hand, everyone is talking and laughing. We are engrossed in a conversation with a most wonderful person. We are wholly present to our friend, indeed, the loved one of our life. All the other chatter, the words, the sounds of glass and ice, and whatever else, are striking our ears, but we are oblivious of them. Our attention is centered. And so it is in the Prayer. But just let someone in a neighboring group mention our name! Suddenly our attention is quite divided, or maybe it has even wholly shifted. It may be a while before our interlocutor again wholly holds our attention. . . . But our Loved One is present. Our attention returns.

We use the prayer word when we need it and to the extent we need it, and always gently. The thoughts and feelings and images will always be there. But it is only when we become *aware* of them, when they have drawn our attention away from the depths, from the Beloved, to themselves, that we need to deliberately—but always gently—employ our prayer word to return to the Presence. For the rest, we let the word simply be there. It may repeat itself, faster or slower, stronger or weaker; it may take up the rhythm of our heart or of our breath (though we do not in any way seek to bring this about, or give any attention to either of these), or it may fuzz out and be more of a silent image than an actual sound. No matter! Our attention is to the Presence, known in faith, embraced in love; the word is incidental, a useful means, used when a means is useful.

In prayer we seek God. We do not seek peace, quiet, tranquillity, enlightenment; we do not seek anything for ourselves. We seek to *give* ourselves, or, rather, we *do* simply give ourselves, even without attending to ourselves, so whole is our intent upon the one to whom we give: *God*. He is the all of our prayer. If thoughts and images and feelings career around in our head and in our heart, little matter. We pay no attention to them. We do not seek to get rid of them any more than we seek to entertain them. As we give ourselves in our loving attention to God, we also give them to him. And let him do with them what he wants to do with them.

And that is the point of them. We will talk more about thoughts in a later chapter, for they seem to be the big question for most persons when they first enter into contemplative prayer. Contemplative prayer does call for a quite different attitude toward thoughts than does active or discursive prayer. Here, in the totality of our gift to God, we simply give him all, even the thoughts and images and feelings that flow through our minds. All are given simply to him to let him do what he wants with them.

Perhaps we have now said enough on the three rules for the moment, except for that second half of the first rule that some prefer to call a fourth rule:

> . . . and at the end of the Prayer we take several minutes to come out, mentally praying the "Our Father" or some other prayer.

We do not want to jump from deep prayer right back into activity. On one level—the physiological—it could be distressing. When we settle down in deep meditation, our whole system settles down: the breathing quiets, the heart slows down, our body almost seems to sleep. *Ego dormio sed cor meum vigilat*—"I sleep, but my heart watches." We want to rise back, gently, to the active level, bringing back with us some of that deep inner quiet and peace, harmony and rhythm.

More important, we want to bring back to the conceptual and affective level what we can of the deep experience of God we have been enjoying. So it is recommended that at the end of our predetermined time of meditation, we move to interior prayer of an affective and conceptual type. Thus the experience we have had is able to find some expression on these levels of our lives and from them flow in a more reflectively experiential way into our ongoing lives.

Over the past months, I have had occasion to share with men and women who have devoted quite a few years to various forms of Eastern meditation, such as TM, who express themselves as experiencing some very real frustration. It seems to arise from an inability to relate the good experience they have been having in meditation with the rest of their lives. Or, another way they express it, their lives, centered on, and in many ways animated by, their meditation practice, do not seem to be responding to their affective needs.

What I see happening is that they are not able to relate the transcendental experience they are having with anything they can perceive on the conceptual level or respond to in an affective way. Their Eastern masters articulate their experience in accord with their own culture and conceptual framework. The average Westerner finds it hard to grasp this and to relate it to the everyday life he or she is called upon to live in our Western society. In many cases, prior to turning East they had written off Christianity or Judaism as not having the answers they need. And so, even though the best of the Eastern masters often tell their disciples to integrate their meditation experience with their own culture and religious background, Western devotees usually do not see this as a possibility unless they are fortunate enough to find a believer who is open to and understands the kind of experience they have been having and is able to help them rediscover their former faith or the Western heritage of faith in the light of the meditative transcendental experience they have enjoyed.

It is important, not only to avoid such frustrations but also to integrate our contemplative experience into our lives, that we be able to relate our experience to a conceptual articulation to which we can respond affectively. The Christian with the historical revelation is in a particularly happy situation in this regard, for the very one whom he or she experiences in the contemplative experience has actually spoken to and made known to him or her the inner reality of what has been experienced, and that in a very personal and loving way: "I no longer call you servants but friends, because I have made known to you all that the Father has made known to me." The inner mystery of the One whom we have touched in our contemplative experience has been articulated for us in so far as it can be. It has been revealed to us in the image of a most loving Father who engenders us as most dear children and gives us the Spirit of Life so that we may adequately respond to his great love as we so desperately need to respond.

We have, then, a real need to relate our experience of God in deep prayer to the other levels of our life. We can begin to do this effectively by moving into affective prayer at the end of our meditation.

The Lord's Prayer seems preeminently suitable for this. This is so not only because it is the prayer that God himself has taught us— the perfect school of prayer—but also because it articulates the essential desires that flow out of a contemplative prayer experience. In going to our deepest self, we get in touch with who we really are —namely, one who has been baptized into Christ, made son with the very Son. And so our whole being cries out: *Father!* "We do not know how to pray as we ought, but the Spirit who has been poured out into our hearts cries, '*Abba*, Father.'"

Experiencing ourselves deeply in God, coming forth from his creative love, we at the same time experience all others coming forth with us from that same creative love. And so we most aptly say: *Our* Father.

We have just experienced him in all his beauty, in all his wonder. Our need is to praise, to affirm, to acclaim. *Hallowed be thy Name.*

The response to such goodness, such beauty, such kindness, can only be love. And love expresses itself in a unity of wills, in wanting what the beloved wants: *Thy Kingdom come, Thy will be done—* yes, even here on earth, with the same perfection and fullness with which it is done in heaven.

And what is God's will? What is the meaning of the whole creation project? Our happiness. God made us to know him so that we might love him, so that we might be happy with him, share in his happiness. There is no other reason for creation. God had all happiness, all goodness. But in the supereminent goodness of his love he wanted others to share it with him. And thus he created—he created us, you and me.

But we must first live: *Give us this day our daily bread.* Out of the universal compassion that comes from knowing our oneness in the creative source of our Father's love, this cry rises up for all the hungry of the earth: "Give us this day our daily bread." But even as we pray in a heartfelt way for the material bread that will sustain human life, we also sense a need and pray for other breads: the bread of wisdom and knowledge and understanding, an ever greater entering into the fullness of the Bread of Truth, the Word of Life that feeds our minds and hearts. And we hunger for the supersubstantial Bread of the Eucharist.

Man must also live in peace, in peace with himself, being at peace with his God, and in peace with his fellowmen: *Forgive us our trespasses as we forgive those who trespass against us.*

And lead us not into temptation, but deliver us from evil, for thine is the Kingdom. How often, coming to this phrase, have I experienced the tensions, the strivings, the concerns of life falling away. His is the kingdom. All is within his domain. "He's got the whole wide world in his hands." I need fear nothing. All is under control.

For thine is the power. It is all going to be taken care of. All will be brought to its predestined fullness. Nothing escapes him or the power of his love. Even my most wayward tendencies, my pride, my ambitions, my lust, my anger, my gluttony—all will come under the reign of his power, till all is brought to perfection, to his glory.

For thine is the glory, for ever and ever. The new depths of life that have been fathomed here are but a beginning—a beginning that will stretch on and on, into the endless day of the Lord. *Amen.*

Each time we come out of the depths and bring their meaning into this school of the Lord's Prayer we will touch some new aspect, some new depth of its meaning. Once, a nun asked St. Teresa how to become a contemplative. The great teacher of prayer replied: "Sister, say the Our Father, but take an hour to say it." We do not propose that one take an hour, but it would be well to freely allow the prayer to unfold, to savor its every phrase, and to let it flow for a bit if it will. Thus the wordless experience of the Infinite Love that is irradiating the deepest parts of our being can slowly surface and spill over, deepening and vitalizing our thoughts and images, calling forth our heart's affection, filling us with an ever greater desire to return again to the depths to experience, to drink from the wellsprings of such life and love.

Although the prayer we use when coming out of our meditation need not necessarily be the Lord's Prayer, I do not think any other is quite so apt. If we are doing the Centering Prayer in conjunction with the Eucharistic Liturgy, as we have often done in Centering Prayer workshops, we might use it as part of the penitential rite. Nothing can put us in touch with our true sinfulness so effectively as this silent standing before the infinitely pure God. And then we might feel that the apt prayer for coming out would be Psalm 130

(129): "Out of the depths I have cried to you, O Lord." Or we might enter into the Prayer after the penitential rite, purified by his mercy, to experience his resplendent goodness and beauty, and come forth with the *Gloria:* Glory to God in the highest. . . .

Some have asked about using the *Hail Mary*. Their deep prayer has been mothering the Christ in their soul. And perhaps they are aware that this grace of prayer that is flowing is, like all the graces that flow into their lives, coming to them through the loving hands of the Mediatrix of all grace.

We can use *any* prayer, a free-flowing prayer in our own words and images—anything that will bring something of the deep experience quietly up into the plane of activity into which we are to move. We will want to speak more about the relationships involved here when we come to speak of the fruits of Centering Prayer. For now, we have perhaps said enough about the method and might profitably turn our attention to some consideration of the theological realities that we live and experience in this Prayer.

APPENDIX

We offer here a few examples of the way the movement of faith and love at the beginning of the Centering Prayer might be expressed. These are only examples of individual expressions. No one should try to use them or imitate them precisely. Each should allow the movement of faith and love to well up from his or her own heart and use those words that spontaneously come to express such a movement.

1. Lord, I believe that you are truly present in me, at the center of my being, bringing me forth in your love. For these few minutes, I want to be completely to you. Draw me, Lord, into your presence. Let me experience your presence and love.

2. Father, I thank you for your wonderful presence. I want to be completely to you in adoration, praise, love, thanksgiving. Let me experience your presence, your love, your care. I come to you, Father, in Christ Jesus, my Lord.

3. Jesus, you are truly present at the center of my being, at the ground of my being. I love you, Lord. I am one with you in your love. Jesus, be my all. Jesus, draw me to yourself. Jesus. Jesus.

V

TO BE WHO WE ARE

We sometimes hear it said that we should read the Scriptures as if they were letters from a loved one. There is a lot to be said for this, yet I do not think it goes far enough. For the One who speaks to us is not far away—by no means. He is more present to us than we are to ourselves, to paraphrase St. Augustine. We ought not to *read* the Scriptures, but *listen* to them, for our Beloved is present and speaks to us through them. That is why they are always so actual. He speaks now, to where we are here and now. An old familiar passage sometimes carries the old familiar message, for that is what we need to hear now, and sometimes it carries a new word of life.

This morning I was listening again to that most beautiful of love songs, the Song of Songs. The Lord and I have been talking a lot about this book, and so as I listened to him this morning he quite naturally spoke to me of Centering Prayer.

FOURTH POEM

I sleep, but my heart is awake.
I hear my Beloved knocking.
"Open to me, my sister, my love,
my dove, my perfect one,
for my head is covered with dew,
my locks with the drops of night."

—"I have taken off my tunic,
am I to put it on again?
I have washed my feet,
am I to dirty them again?"

My Beloved thrust his hand
through the opening in the door;
I trembled to the core of my being.
Then I rose
to open to my Beloved,
myrrh ran off my hands,
pure myrrh off my fingers,
on to the handle of the bolt.

I opened to my Beloved,
but he had turned his back and gone!
My soul failed at his flight.
I sought him but I did not find him,
I called to him but he did not answer.
The watchmen came upon me
as they made their rounds in the City.
They beat me, they wounded me,
they took away my cloak,
they who guard the ramparts.

—Sg. 5:2–7

"I sleep, but my heart is awake." How well that describes the experience of Centering Prayer! All within quiets down—it is very much like going to sleep—but our hearts are very vigilant, attentive, present to him who is present at the core, at the center of our being. He is there constantly, and yet in a way he is not there. He is not present to us as human beings are, as men and women made present by love, until we open to him. This brought to my mind a passage from the Book of Revelation that speaks so powerfully to me, and on which I have commented in the first chapter of this book: "Behold, I stand at the door and knock; if anyone hears my voice and opens the door I will come in to share his meal, side by side with him." Centering Prayer is an opening, a response, a putting aside of all the debris that stands in the way of our being totally present to the present Lord, so that he can be present to us. It is a laying aside of thoughts, so that the heart can attend immediately to him.

All prayer is a response. The Lord first knocks, beckons, calls to us. He calls us forth in our very creation and in our re-creation in baptism. He speaks to us in everyone and in everything, in our very selves, in all our movements, energies, and activities, in our breathing, thinking, and feeling. He is the source of all energy, life, and activity, and he is present in them as their source. With a lively faith we hear him and we respond.

Centering Prayer is a good school, where we can begin to learn the kind of listening that enables us to hear the Lord in all and to be responsive to his loving, creative presence and thus come to that constant prayer to which we are called. Some have at times objected to using a method or technique in prayer, for fear that in so doing they might be guilty of trying to manipulate God. What they fail to realize is that the method and the very thought of using it come from the Lord. It is a way by which he calls, knocks. We use a method in prayer because he has given it to us, and with it, the grace to use it; it is all response, a response that fully accepts the incarnation.

When the Lord calls us, he brings the grace we have need of to respond—his own grace which overflows upon us: ". . . my head is covered with dew, my locks with the drops of night." But so often, despite the call, despite the overflowing grace, we are slow to respond. We are comfortably settled. Everything is OK. Perhaps we have established a comfortable routine of prayers and pious exercises. We are settled, comfy in our own little beds. We do not want to rise and open to the mysteries of the night, to a new and more intimate encounter with the Beloved, which may make we know not what kind of demands upon us. Love can be so demanding; in fact, of its very nature it is totally demanding. "I have taken off my tunic, am I to put it on again? I have washed my feet, am I to dirty them again?"

But happily our Beloved is insistent: "My Beloved thrust [a strong word] his hand through the opening in the door." Our Lord is an insistent lover, yet a respectful one. He does not push his way into our lives. There was an opening in the door through which he could thrust his hand. Even if we had not yet opened, we were at least listening. And when we listen, he touches us. And when he touches—"I trembled to the core of my being." His word is a two-edged sword that pierces to the very marrow of the bone.

We need to listen regularly to the Scriptures. It is there that he touches us, rouses us, calls us forth from our settled ways to truly seek him in Centering Prayer. It is the Scriptures, especially the Gospels, that create in us the attentiveness of a loving, desiring heart.

Traditionally, myrrh has been the symbol of suffering; here, the sweet suffering of great desire: "Then I rose to open to my Beloved, myrrh ran off my hands, pure myrrh off my fingers, onto the handle of the bolt." Centering Prayer, a practical handle for opening to the Lord, will be endued with suffering, that sweet suffering of desire. We will open to our Beloved; we will leave behind all the thoughts and images that give us comfortable assurance and warmth, and seek only him, and then—he who had knocked, invited so insistently, is gone; there is no sight of him. He seems to have totally disappeared: "I opened to my Beloved, but he had turned his back and gone!"

Perhaps the words that follow describe what is our most common experience in Centering Prayer: "My soul failed at his flight. I sought him but I did not find him; I called him [at times the use of the prayer word might seem to us more like a cry in the dark than a gentle return to the Presence] but he did not answer."

And our very practical reason, that guardian of common sense and rationality, that knows nothing of love or of the transcendent realities of the realm of faith, will be quick to pounce upon us: "The watchmen came upon me as they made their rounds in the City. They beat me, they wounded me. [Why all this nonsense? Why all this waste of time? There is nothing going on here. There is no one here. You are chasing after your own illusions.] They took away my cloak, they who guarded the ramparts." Yes, reason will batter us and challenge us, and ultimately leave us stripped, to be before the Lord in naked faith—but it is only in such nakedness that we are ready to receive the fullness of the Divine Embrace.

The Greek Fathers have a very beautiful expression: "God became man so that man might become God." The full theological content of that terse phrase could hardly be exhausted. One thing it tells us is that our developing relationship with God is not unlike the development of our more complete human relationships. Indeed, God himself, in speaking to us in the Scriptures, frequently compares his relationship with us to that of a pair of lovers or a husband and wife. When a young man finds a woman with whom he hopes to develop that fullest and most beautiful of human relationships which we call marriage, if he and his beloved are to succeed they must go about it with some seriousness. The couple will spend a lot of time together. At first they will have a lot to talk about. They will seek to disclose to each other something of their mystery as it has revealed itself in the unfolding of their lives and the development of their respective personalities. They will do a lot of things together and for each other. But as the relationship develops they will learn to be together in silence, to commune at a deeper level, to let each other's presence speak, to trust the truthfulness of each other's presence without having to be constantly assured by words. Perhaps one of the causes of the breakup of many marriages in our time is the inability of many to come to this level of communication. They rely so totally on verbal communication that when at length they are talked out, they see nowhere to go and so terminate the relationship and seek someone else with whom to talk. That is perhaps a gross oversimplification of the matter, but there is some truth to it.

In any case, in the normal development of our relationship with our Lord, at first there is usually a lot of verbal communication. Faith comes through hearing. God reveals himself first to us through his Word. We listen to that Word, receive it, let it be in us and grow in us, as it reveals the presence, the love, the goodness and beauty of our God. As we hear the Lord speak to us, we respond with appropriate thoughts and words and acts. We begin to carry the Lord with us more consciously as we go about our daily tasks; his Presence to us becomes more and more constant. We begin to sense the need just to be with him in silence.

A married couple spend a lot of time together. If they really love each other, they are not absent from each other's thoughts even when they are separated. They do a lot of things together, they do things with others, they do things for each other. But if their marriage is to be a success, there have to be times when they are by themselves and leave off all doing and simply are to each other in the marital embrace. At such times neither words nor thoughts are significant. If they are present they are inconsequential—perhaps just a love word to reinforce the fullness of presence.

In our relationship with God, too, beyond all doing and talking and thinking there need to be times when we are simply present to him in the fullness of our being, experiencing the immediacy of his loving and life-giving presence to us. At such times there may still be thoughts and words, but they are inconsequential. We may use a prayer word, a love word to reinforce the presence, but it is the immediate presence of the Lord, or the Lord in his immediate presence, that is the focus of all our attention, of our heart's desire being fulfilled.

And this is our Beloved's delight. Perhaps one of the things that most undermine the development of our intimate relationship with God is our inability to realize and accept the fact that God does really want an intimate relationship with us, that we are really important to him. He made us for no other reason than to enjoy us and to have us enjoy him. He had an absolute fullness of happiness and he wanted to share it, so he made us. Such absolute gratuity is difficult for us to comprehend. Our whole training and the attitudes that prevail in today's world reinforce the conviction that one has to merit love, that everything we get has to be paid for. Not so with God. Nothingness cannot merit until it is gratuitously given something to serve as a basis of activity and possible merit.

God in his great love does give us the ability and the glory of meriting. But, ultimately, all is gift. And so he says: "Unless you become as little children you shall not enter into the Kingdom." Unless we are, like little children, wholly without thought of any deserts, able to accept all from our Father, we cannot hope to have anything. God is our Father, and as a most loving Father he takes delight in us. And he wants us to take delight, to take pride in him, to turn to him for security, love, and care.

A father is delighted when his little one, leaving off his toys and his friends, runs to him and climbs into his arms. As he holds his little one close to him, he cares little whether his child is looking around, his attention flitting from one thing to another, or if he is intent upon his father, or just settling down to sleep. Essentially the child is choosing to be with his father, confident of the love, the care, the security that is his in those arms.

Our Centering Prayer is much like that. We settle down in our Father's arms, in his loving hands. Our mind, our thoughts, our imagination may flit about here and there; we might even fall asleep; but essentially we are choosing to remain for this time intimately with our Father, giving ourselves to him, receiving his love and care, letting him enjoy us as he will. It is very simple prayer. It is very childlike prayer. It is prayer that opens out to us all the delights of the Kingdom. If we do employ a prayer word, it is not so much as a concept or an expression of the mind as a thing of the heart, of the will—an expression of love. It is the Prayer of the Heart.

But what is going on here? It is an affirmation—not so much by word or thought or even understanding in any full sense, but by being—of what actually is: of who God is, who we are, and what is the relationship between us. It is a wholehearted entering into the true relationship that exists between God and ourselves in virtue of who we are by creation and re-creation. It is a total assent to be who we are.

Thomas Merton, in a book he considered one of his best, *New Seeds of Contemplation,* has what I think is an exceptionally beautiful passage:

> A tree gives glory to God by being a tree. For in being what God means it to be it is obeying him. It "consents," so to speak, to his creative love. It is expressing an idea which is in God and which is not distinct from the essence of God, and therefore a tree imitates God by being a tree. (p. 29)

By our creation we, too, express an idea that is in God, that always has been and always will be and that is not distinct from his very essence. We indeed imitate God, and in a fuller way than anything else in creation. And because we are the kind of creatures that we are, human persons with knowing minds and choosing hearts, and with free will, we can consent to God's creative love not only in a "so to speak" way but in a very godlike way.

Yet there is something far more significant still, for we who have been baptized have not only been created, we have been re-created. Our participation is not—like that of the rest of creation—a sort of extrinsic sharing in the life, the being, the beauty of God. We have been baptized into the very life and love of the Son. "I live, now not I, but Christ lives in me." In some very real way, we have been made one with the very Son of God. And the Spirit of the Son, the Holy Spirit, has been given to us to be our spirit. We have been brought into the inner life of the most Holy Trinity.

The whole being of the Son is from the Father and to the Father in the Holy Spirit. As sons and daughters, one with the very Son, this is the essential movement of our being. We do not know how to pray as we ought, we do not know how to be to the Father in the way that is appropriate and worthy of him, but the Holy Spirit has been poured into our hearts and cries, "*Abba*, Father." This is our essential being as men and women baptized into Christ, made partakers of the Divine Sonship. When we leave off all our superficial activity, when we leave behind our thoughts, our feelings, our flow of images, and simply settle down to assent wholly to being who we are, we are essentially *prayer*—response to God, and a response that is truly worthy of him, for our response is that very Person of Love, the Love of the Son for the Father and of the Father for the Son— the most Holy Spirit of Love.

Saint John of the Cross speaks of this several times in his writings:

> By his divine breath-like spiration, the Holy Spirit elevates the soul sublimely and informs her and makes her capable of breathing in God the same spiration of love that the Father breathes in the Son and the Son in the Father, which is the Holy Spirit himself, who in the Father and the Son breathes out to her in this transformation, in order to unite her to himself. . . . For the soul united and trans- formed in God breathes out in God to God the very divine spiration

which God—she being transformed in him—breathes out in himself in her.—*Spiritual Canticle*, 79:3

Having been made one with God, the soul is somehow God through participation. . . . God is indeed its own and it possesses him by inheritance, with the right of ownership, as his adopted son, through the grace of his gift of himself. Having him for its own, it can give him and communicate him to whomever it wishes. Thus it gives him to its Beloved, who is the very God who gave himself to it. By this donation it repays God for all it owes him, since it willingly gives as much as it receives from him.

Because the soul in this gift to God offers him the Holy Spirit, with voluntary surrender, as something of its own (so that God loves himself in the Holy Spirit as he deserves), it enjoys inestimable delight and fruition, seeing that it gives God something of its own which is suited to him according to his infinite being.—*The Living Flame of Love*, 3:78f.

This is a most perfect prayer, beyond which nothing greater can ever be conceived. And it is this prayer that we essentially seek to enter into and be wholly present to when we enter into Centering Prayer. A friend of mine, a minister, expressed this in a more concrete and down-to-earth way:

I've found that the only way I can really function is from that root-edness, or centeredness. . . . I don't subscribe to a "God-out-in-the-sky" kind of idea. Perhaps the Christian doctrine of the Incarnation would be the best explanation I could give—God in the flesh, bringing that potential not just to one man, Jesus, but to every man. For me, Jesus has shown in his human flesh how one can live with unconditional love and oneness and serving. I look at the example of Jesus and I realize that this is *my* possibility. . . . We are created in the image and likeness of God, but running our patterns, playing our games, and having our acts prevents us from living out the fullness of who we are.

Cardinal Suhard, to whom I owe an eternal debt for having first awakened in me some realization of the vast and exciting implications of what it means to be a Christian, very concisely brings together the theological sources for the reality we are seeking to be in touch with in Centering Prayer:

> God, by the fact of their creation, is present in all creatures. "In him we live, move and have our being," says St. Paul (Ac. 17:28). In some splendid pages of the *Summa*, St. Thomas takes up this statement of "God existing in all things": "As long as a thing has being . . . it is a necessary conclusion from this that God is in all things and in an intimate way" (I:8:1). What, then, must we say of God's presence by grace in the soul, a presence which is not merely that of God the Creator immanent in his creature, but the intimacy of the three Divine Persons shared with us? "We will come and make our dwelling place there" (Jn. 14:23).—Pastoral Letter: *The Meaning of God in the Church Today*.

St. Augustine, with his usual forcefulness and daring, states the matter in a way that betrays some of his own excitement:

> Let us applaud and give thanks that we have become not only Christians but Christ himself. Do you understand, my brothers, the grace that God our head has given us? Be filled with wonder and joy—we have become veritable Christs.

If we are really one with Christ (the fact of Baptism), and Christ is now sitting at the Father's right hand, then we are truly in heaven and at the Father's right. The rest is illusion? No. Because Christ is also really here—everywhere. Everywhere, but nowhere, but there at the Father's right. When we come to the center, to our truest selves, we are where Christ most truly is. "I and the Father are one." "You, Father, are in me and I in you." We are not just in heaven, just at the Father's right, but *in* the Father, within the Godhead, within the Trinity, within the movement of Love, the torrential cascade of Love that is the Spirit, flowing from Father to Son and from Son to Father and wholly embracing them and engulfing them and us in the one Love.

When we go to the center, we leave behind time and place and separateness. We come to our Source and are in the Being from which we ever flow and in which we ever stand and apart from which we are not. All is yet in the mystery of the Reality. It is not just being, but it is Trinity, and we are loved and we love. There is a communication and a certain communion of Persons, of Lovers. And into this we all have been baptized. Can we ever fully comprehend what baptism really means? No! "I live, no, now not I, but Christ lives in me." Not in us as in a place, but in us as being. Our being is Christ's being—in some way—oh, incomprehensible way! It is best just simply to go to the center and let it all be, and be experienced, and not try to say what it is all about!

The reality of what is, of who we are, is so tremendously wonderful. The sad thing is that most of us are running away from our own reality. We experience our contingency and desperately want to create or find something on which we can depend. Unfortunately we look in the wrong direction. We look outside ourselves, or seek to construct a false self, a very fragile shell, whose all-too-obvious fragility leaves us in a constant state of fear and defensiveness. We need to reverse our direction and to see and accept our true selves. With the discovery that our contingency rests on a God of infinite love, intimately present, what security, what affirmation we experience! God's love for us is proved by the greatest of proofs: he sent his Son to be crucified for us. "God so loved the world, he sent his Son." And what could be more affirming than the fact that at every moment the infinite God is present to us, bringing us forth in his creative love? If we are so loved by God, how lovable we must be!

Merton, in the last book which he personally prepared for publication, *The Climate of Monastic Prayer*, expresses this powerfully:

> First of all, our meditation should begin with the realization of our nothingness and helplessness in the presence of God. This need not be a mournful or discouraging experience. On the contrary, it can be deeply tranquil and joyful, since it brings us in direct contact with the source of all joy and all life. But one reason why our meditation never gets started is that perhaps we never make this real, serious return to the center of our own nothingness before God. Hence we never enter into the deepest reality of our relationship with him.
>
> In other words, we meditate merely "in the mind," in the imagination, or at best in the desires, considering religious truths from a de-

tached objective viewpoint. We do not begin by seeking to "find our heart"—that is, to sink into a deep awareness of the ground of our identity before God and in God. "Finding our heart" and recovering this awareness of our inmost identity implies the recognition that our external everyday self is to a great extent a mask and a fabrication. It is not our true self. And indeed our true self is not easy to find. It is hidden in obscurity and "nothingness" at the center where we are in direct dependence on God. But since the reality of all Christian meditation depends on this recognition, our attempt to meditate without it is in fact self-contradictory. It is like trying to walk without feet.

This is the first step of the Centering Prayer method: going beyond the false self and all that constructs it, returning to the center, getting in touch with what is, being what is. Once we are there, we are prayer. By accepting to be who we are, we pray. There is nothing more. And there could be nothing more. For we have entered into the fullness of God.

Why, then, a method? The method of Centering Prayer is like a trellis. It is of the very nature of a climbing rose to reach up toward the sun and blossom forth. But without a trellis it keeps falling back on itself, and soon we have a large knotted mass that does not rise very high and gives birth to very few blooms. But if the climbing rose is given the support of a trellis, it can reach up and up toward the sun—the Sun of Justice and Life—and bear an ever greater abundance of blossoms.

The Centering Prayer method simply helps us to remain in the true movement of who we are; and each time we fall back on ourselves, it enables us to return to that reality. The quiet, gentle, constant, though ofttimes imperceptible presence of our prayer word, our word of love, is the trellis. And when we do begin to fall back on ourselves, when we become *aware* that we are attending to something other than God—in other words, when we have returned to self-awareness and are again watching what we are doing instead of being intent upon simply being who we are and being wholly alert in the movement of that reality, being the Son to the Father in the Love that is the Holy Spirit—our trellis, our prayer word, gently reaches out to return us to the freedom of being wholly at one in our direction, in our movement of love.

We are here touching on the third rule, and there is something here that is sometimes difficult to grasp as one moves from active prayer to this more passive, contemplative type of prayer. In active prayer our thoughts, and ofttimes our imagination, are fully engaged in the prayer itself—or should be. And any thought or image that comes along that is not part of the prayer is a distraction, something that takes us away from the prayer. But in contemplative prayer, or the Prayer of the Heart, we are responding to God at a different level. I do not mean to say by this that the heart, the will, is not present in active prayer. It is—very much so—but very much in and through thoughts and images. In Centering Prayer the heart is directly reaching to God, immediately present at the center, the ground of our being. The thoughts and images, after their initial participation, have nothing to do with the heart's prayer.

Do you remember the story our Lord told about the bridesmaids waiting for the bridegroom? As he tarried, they slumbered. When he arrived, five with their lamps burning were ready for him; five with their lamps now dead were not. The five whose lamps kept burning, even while they slept were yet waiting, were attentive; the fire of their love for the groom was ever burning. The other five, their love extinguished, no longer waited; they simply slept.

Have you ever waited eagerly for someone? As you waited, you might have engaged in conversation with others, you might have read or distracted yourself in one way or another, you might have dozed, but always your ear was to the door. The least sound there immediately brought you to full attention. Your real attention, your heart, was never with the one you conversed with or the task that filled the time; it was always with the one coming.

I can remember one morning sitting on a pier on the north coast of Athos, awaiting the boat that would take me back to the mainland. As I waited—having no idea how long the wait might be—I occupied myself with writing in my journal. But my attention was ever on the coming boat, on the promontory around which it would eventually appear. Any least movement in that direction, any sound that even faintly resembled the sound of the little motor launch, immediately brought my eyes from the paper to the promontory. My fingers may well have been busy writing, my thoughts may have been on the things I was writing about, but my heart was set upon something else.

This is much how it is in the Prayer of the Heart or Centering Prayer. It certainly is an immense joy when our prayer is integral, when our mind is quiet, our imagination stilled, and all our being in harmony with the resting of our heart in God. But that is not so often the case. Indeed, I think that is a rather special gift from the Lord, something to be truly enjoyed and relished when it is given. But in actual fact it is not always the best thing for us and that is why the Lord does not always allow us to enjoy it. Much of the time, while we set our hearts upon the Lord, our mind and imagination amuse themselves and fill the time with their own devices. Little matter. We need not concern ourselves about it. Our heart is set upon the Lord. We are in deep prayer, in heart-to-heart communion with our Lord. We may not have the same sense of satisfaction we might have if we could sense a peace and an integralness. But we do not pray for our own satisfaction. We pray in response to God's great love, to give our hearts to him. The rest is inconsequential. If thoughts or images—or anything else—from time to time or seemingly much of the time, do seek to draw us away from our heart's attention, or actually do—no matter. With our prayer word, we gently turn back to our Beloved, and have the merit of this additional choice for God, this additional explicit act of love.

One thing we can see here: the importance of going to prayer simply to be to God without any expectations. If we go to prayer looking for or expecting an experience of some sort, to find peace or quiet, if we are concerned about doing it right, getting the right effect or result, then we are no longer simply seeking God. We are in some way seeking ourselves, seeking something for ourselves, and we cannot simply *be* to God. We cannot wholly enter into the essential movement of our being. We cannot really succeed in Centering Prayer. We are seeking something that pertains to our more superficial selves, and thus we divide our attention and keep one eye fixed on ourselves and our own gain, satisfaction, and accomplishment. Centering Prayer is very simple, very pure, and for that reason very demanding, indeed totally demanding. We should not go to the Prayer seeking to achieve something, to succeed in making a Centering Prayer, in doing it right. We simply seek to be to God and let happen what may. Here Dom Chapman's oft-repeated words are relevant: "Pray as you can, don't pray as you can't."

As the Centering Prayer Movement grew, we gradually developed an Advanced Centering Prayer Retreat-Workshop. In this particular type of workshop the participants do a great deal of centering. In the course of the afternoon alone, they have four successive meditations, with a short meditative walk between successive sessions. In the evening the participants share openly their experience in the day's meditations. This has its dangers, for as we have said, everything that goes on in the course of our centering apart from our simple attention to God is quite irrelevant. There is little or nothing we can say about our simple attention to God, and so the participants share mostly about the irrelevant. But such sharing does have a beneficial effect. It strongly brings home through the extensive sharing during the week how varied are the things that can happen when one is centering and yet how truly irrelevant it all is. Let me quote one person's report of an afternoon's experience:

> The afternoon was interesting. The first meditation was good. I had hardly any thoughts. While we were out taking the walk I thought, this is going to be a good day. But little did I know. When we came back and sat down for the second meditation the beginning was all right. Then I began to hear music: the *1812 Overture*. It was in my head. Finally it faded and the rest was kind of quiet. So we went out and walked again. Then when we returned for the third one, it hit me. We talked about tornadoes. Everything went off and at one point I started to feel very guilty. That got more intense and then I began to feel sad. And then all of a sudden the sadness left and I felt very joyful. In the middle of the third—or was it the fourth?—it was just like heaven. . . .

After hearing a dozen or so reports like this from our fellow meditators night after night, we begin to realize that just about anything is apt to happen, that no one meditation is a prognosis of what the following one might be like, that we would best have no expectations but simply wait upon the Lord and let happen what happens.

Among the Syrian Jews there is a series of stories about a very lovable old fellow by the name of Mullernestredon. One day this good man was seen busily searching in the village square, around the trees, under the carts, behind the trash cans. A sympathetic friend approached and asked if he had lost something. "Yes, my key," he answered. The friend joined in the search. After several fruitless and frustrating hours, the friend began to interrogate the old man: "Are you sure you lost your key here in the square? Where did you last see it?" "On the table in my house," was the reply. "Then, why in the name of the heavens are you looking for it out here?" "Because there is more light out here."

Like Mullernestredon, we often look for God in our thoughts and imaginings, our feelings and affections, because they seem to us more lightsome. But that is not where he is ultimately to be found. He is to be found in the depths of our being, at the center, at the ground of our being, perceived by the searching light of faith or the knowing embrace of love. All the feelings, thoughts, and images that float around in our prayer do not really put us in touch with him. These are "out in the square." He is within. And there we are so one with him that we are communion, union, prayer.

There is another story told of a rabbi—Rabbi Zuscha. On his deathbed he was asked what he thought the Kingdom of God would be like. The old Rabbi thought for a long time; then he replied: "I don't really know. But one thing I do know: When I get there, I am not going to be asked, 'Why weren't you Moses?' or 'Why weren't you David?' I am going to be asked, 'Why weren't you Zuscha?'"

This is what Centering Prayer aims at: being who we really are, who we really are in virtue of what happened to us at Baptism: the Son to the Father in the Holy Spirit, which is perfect love, which is perfect prayer.

VI

THOUGHTS, THOUGHTS, AND MORE THOUGHTS

As we enter into the practice of Centering Prayer and acquire an understanding of it, perhaps no other area causes as much difficulty as does that of thoughts. This is not surprising. We belong to a tradition that has commonly defined man as a rational animal—the thinking one. Thought is highly prized and richly rewarded, whether it be the practical thinking of the scientist, the economist, or sociologist, or the creative thinking of the litterateur. Many of the methods of prayer that have predominated in recent centuries in our Western tradition have laid great stress on thoughts and images. Where there was more openness to feelings and emotions, these were to be aroused in response to the word of faith.

Moreover, it would undoubtedly be easier for us to handle the problem of thoughts if Centering Prayer, like Quietism, just called for the suppression of thoughts. But it does not. Rather, it calls for a dispossessiveness, a detachment from something we have so intimately identified with ourselves—"I think, therefore I am"—and letting Another use our thoughts: having them and yet having them not.

So it would be good to take a few minutes to consider carefully the role of thoughts in this type of prayer.

To facilitate our discussion I would like to distinguish five kinds of thoughts. Actually they are not really distinct from each other, and certainly in practice we should not concern ourselves with trying to put the thoughts we encounter in our Prayer in one or another particular class. This is merely a construct to clarify presentation.

First of all, we might speak of *the simple thought*, one of the millions that flow steadily through our mind, with greater or lesser accompanying imagery, emotional overtones, and physical stimulation. There is indeed a constant stream of such thoughts flowing through all our waking hours. When we enter into our Prayer, the stream flows on. But we quietly sink into the depths beneath them and just let them flow along while we abide in the center with God.

Now, as we let go and settle in the deep movement of the stream of prayer, from time to time—and sometimes it seems to us it is *all* the time—things grab at us, thoughts or images, feelings or noises, and they pull us up out of the depths to the surface as they imperiously demand our attention.

We might call this second kind of thought *the catching thought*. It is the one that angles down into the depths, hooks us, and pulls us back to the surface. This is where our third rule applies: "Whenever in the course of the Prayer we become *aware* of anything else, we simply gently return to the Presence by the use of the prayer word."

This return by means of the prayer word should be very gentle, very simple. If we make a big deal of it, or begin to get annoyed with ourselves for having had the catching thought, we will only succeed in drawing ourselves farther away from the center and more onto the surface.

Suppose I am standing and talking with you on the ninth floor of a building. Suddenly there is a great commotion on the street below which disturbs our conversation. If I leave the room, take the elevator down to the lobby, and go out onto the street to tell everybody to be quiet, I have only succeeded in interrupting our conversation far more drastically. Rather, I need simply to redirect my attention to our conversation and go on with it.

When I want to swim underwater I need lots of air. I take some very full inhalations before I dive into the pool. Then, when I need more air, I simply surface, take a quick breath, and go on in my underwater journey. Each time I need a breath I do not climb out of the pool and fully renew my original hyperventilation. So, too, in the Prayer. At the beginning, in order to move to the center, I make explicit acts of faith and love. But once I am in the Prayer, each time I am drawn out by a *catching thought* I do not begin to repeat my whole original movement of faith and love. Rather, with my prayer word, which capsulates the fullness of my faith-love relationship with God, present in me, I very gently renew my prayer by returning to the Presence at the center.

The third kind of thought I call *the monitor*, and it is by far the most troublesome. In active or discursive meditation, we perhaps choose a scene from the Gospel—for example, the women meeting the Risen Lord on their way. We ponder on this scene, on our Lord's words, the women's reactions. We seek to enter more deeply into the meaning, arouse affections, develop motivation, make resolutions. When our prayer is over we can look back and reflect: Yes, I had a good meditation today. I had good thoughts, made good acts of the will, came up with some good resolutions. Or, I had a terrible meditation today; lots of distractions, felt completely dead.

What does this tell me? It tells me that the whole time I was praying or meditating, though I might have had one eye on God, I had the other one on myself, keeping careful account of what I was doing. This is *the monitor*, that eye on self, or really self itself.

The purity of Centering Prayer lies in this: for once, both eyes are on God. For the first time, perhaps, we are beginning to fulfill the first great commandment: "Love the Lord your God with your *whole* mind. . . ." But self does not want to do this; it wants to keep one eye on itself—the monitor. The whole evaluating system of our culture and society supports it. We are very production-oriented. To do something and not keep track of what is coming out of it is very alien to our usual way of functioning, even in prayer. We find our value and affirm the worth of ourselves, our activities, and our very existence, according to our productivity. To let go and forget about producing and just be and enjoy is a natural gift we have virtually lost. We go about even our recreations and vacations with a certain deadly earnestness. If we are able at times actually to relax and just enjoy a beer or a cup of coffee with a friend, or abandon ourselves to deeper expressions of love without immediately questioning ourselves about their productivity, it is because we have convinced ourselves that in the long run such experiences and spaces are necessary for the overall balance of a truly productive life.

There is another factor here. There is no more effective way to destroy someone than to ignore him simply and totally. When we fight someone or get angry with him, we at least affirm his existence and to some extent his significance. But when we completely ignore him, he simply ceases to exist for us.

Self—the false, superficial, reporting self—does not want to cease to exist, does not want to die. So *the monitor* is there, trying to keep an eye on what is going on, to affirm self's presence and productivity. As we enter into the Centering Prayer, if all is going well and we are settling peacefully in the Lord, *the monitor* will soon be asking: "How did I get here? What precisely did I do, so I can be sure to do this again tomorrow?" Or: "I wonder if I am doing this all right? Am I doing as well as this one next to me? What will I be able to say about this? What am I getting out of this?" Et cetera.

Here again we have to apply the third rule, and with a certain ruthlessness; in fact, the more ruthlessly the better. *The monitor*, the servant of false self-love and pride, is going to put up a long fight before he dies. He will be the most relentless enemy of Centering Prayer, because he wants to be himself at the center. Centering Prayer is very simple, but it is not easy, precisely because it does involve the death to self—the false, fabricated self—in order to be able to be and to live wholly unto God. Nobody wants to die!

The fourth kind of thought I call *the bright idea*. People who are creative are most prone to this one. Also, those in ministry. We enter into the Prayer, and all of a sudden there it is: the whole sermon is worked out, the problem we have been tussling with is solved, the design is complete, the chapter is written, and so forth. We know that in sleep, while on one level we are enjoying deep rest, the mind can still be working, and with greater freedom, on another level, and succeed in bringing things together. So, too, in deep prayer. However, if during the time of the Prayer we do seize upon the bright idea, the solution, the design, and, leaving our Prayer, begin to work with it, I think we will usually find it is actually only half-baked. If we faithfully follow the third rule, let the bright idea go and continue with our Prayer, the idea will emerge again later, outside of prayer, and in a completed state, ready to serve us.

Be that as it may, the important thing is fidelity to the Prayer, and in this fidelity is the experiential affirmation of the value of prayer in itself, namely, that prayer is not production-oriented but, rather, the beginning of heaven, the simple enjoyment of God, the reality for which he made us.

There will surface during Centering Prayer insights into ourselves, our weaknesses, passions, desires, self-deceptions. The time set apart for our Prayer is not the time to work with these. If we are faithful to our Prayer, letting these insights go at that time, we will find they will resurface more clearly and fully at the proper time—during examen or when talking with our spiritual father or mother. And then we will be in the situation and have the grace to work with them. If we leave off our prayer and begin working with them out of season, we might well find ourselves in trouble. Besides coping with the insights, we will also have to cope with their accompanying tensions, from which the Lord had intended to free us in the course of our Prayer.

This brings us to our fifth kind of thought, *the stressful thought.* As I said at the beginning of this chapter, these five kinds of thoughts are not to be wholly distinguished one from another. Indeed, oftentimes the thoughts we have already considered will also be *stressful thoughts;* that is, thoughts that arise out of relations and situations that are causing or have caused tension in our lives.

There are certain parallels between deep prayer and sleep. That is why St. Teresa would say, "When some first enter into the Prayer of Quiet they have many misgivings—they wonder if they are really praying, or if anything at all is going on, or if they are not just falling asleep. . . ." When we enter into contemplative prayer we, as it were, enter into another state of consciousness. For most of us, the only other experience we have had of such a passing has been falling asleep, passing from the waking to the sleeping state. As we know, apart from using artificial means such as drugs, we cannot make ourselves go to sleep. In fact, the more we try, the less apt we are to succeed. It is, rather, by disposing ourselves, setting up apt conditions, and letting go, that we best succeed. And so it is with contemplative, or deep, prayer. And that is precisely what the Centering Prayer method is: a very simple and effective means of disposing ourselves and setting up an apt situation so that we can pass or be drawn from our ordinary self-reflective state to one of pure consciousness (to use an expression Merton often employed), when we can be simply present to reality—God and all that is in and of God—in an undivided way. Any effort on our part to produce such a state will only throw us back more on ourselves and have the opposite effect to that which we are seeking.

But there is another similarity between sleep and deep prayer. Those who have studied the matter in the behavioral-science laboratories tell us that when a normal person sleeps, he or she has a great many dreams, whether they are remembered or not. By observing rapid eye motion, the scientist can tell when the person is entering into the dream state. It is possible to keep a sleeping person from having dreams by stimulating him gently each time he begins to move into the dream state. But these scientists have established in their experiments that if they consistently prevent a person from dreaming even for a relatively short period of time—a few nights—the person is very apt to undergo a psychotic episode. Dreams are an important means by which the sleeper releases the tension that has been building up in his or her life.

There is here a parallel between the role of dreams and the role of the thoughts that flow through our mind during deep prayer. Just as dreams release tension from our lives while we sleep, so too do thoughts and images that flow through our minds while we are resting in contemplative prayer.

Now it is precisely those thoughts and feelings which are most stressful that have the greatest hold on us, that are most apt to hook us and pull us up out of our prayer. If we respond to the thought or feeling or image and begin working with it, we increase the tension it is causing. But if at the moment we become *aware* of the thought we can simply let it go by, gently returning to the center with our prayer word, the tension will flow out of our lives.

It is in this way that the Lord refreshes us even psychologically during our deep prayer. God allows thoughts, feelings, memories, and images to flow across the surface of our mind during prayer so that he can use them to free us from built-up tension. The important thing is that we let go and let him use them. In contemplative prayer, thoughts and images are no longer our business. They are his. We are all his. We let go and simply let him enter in and take over and do what he wants to do in our life and in our prayer.

Thus, when we enter into the way of contemplative prayer, we have to undergo a real conversion of attitude toward thoughts. In an active prayer, such as discursive meditation, thought is very much a part of our prayer. And any thought that is not actively a part of the prayer is a distraction, something drawing us away from the prayer, something bad. From such past experience we are apt to have a real prejudice against thoughts: Any thoughts *we* are not using in our prayer are bad. And since in contemplative prayer we do not use any thoughts, all thoughts are bad—something to be deplored, something to be fought. But this is wrong. In contemplative prayer there are no distractions. There are thoughts, and they are good—if only we let them go and let God use them the way he wants to use them.

This is the degree to which we must die to ourselves in Centering Prayer. Not even our own thoughts can be considered our own. They must all be given over to the Lord to let him use them as he wishes. Far from decrying them or seeing them as something bad, their worth is greatly affirmed, as they are considered worthy of being offered to the Lord and used by him. Centering Prayer does not deny the value of thoughts and images, but it assigns to them a different role, a different way of enabling us to go beyond them to the reality they seek to express, to a fuller freedom, a purer and more intimate union. So—thoughts, thoughts, and more thoughts. . . . Let them flow, let them go, go beyond them to the Reality!

VII

PROGRESS IN CENTERING PRAYER

I would like to share with you three reactions to Centering Prayer:

Recently I led a workshop on Centering Prayer for seminary spiritual directors. After an initial presentation, one of the spiritual directors asked: Is this the kind of prayer we should move our directees toward, with the idea that when they get there they will stay there?

On another occasion, a young religious was sharing with me his experience in prayer. After his first few experiences in contemplative prayer, he said, he asked himself: Is this all there is to it?

Finally, a priest who had been centering regularly for several years wrote to me from Rome shortly after his election as superior general of his congregation: "As for the Prayer, all I can say is that when I miss it, *I miss it.*"

It seems to me that that spiritual director who was not yet well acquainted with or practiced in experiential prayer was still approaching prayer as a project. This is most common. In our accomplishment-oriented society we tend to approach everything as a project—something to be done, accomplished. There is a determined, measurable finished product. In prayer the program is lined up according to the traditional teaching. If we are in touch with the more ancient teaching, we think in terms of *lectio, meditatio, oratio, contemplatio*—receiving the Word of faith through listening or *reading,* internalizing it by a faith-response in discursive or imaginative *meditation,* responding to it in living, affective *prayer,* and finally enjoying it in quiet *contemplation.* We may be sophisticated enough to know that no one of these four will ordinarily occur as a pure state or way of prayer. There will usually be an admixture. As, for example, in Centering Prayer: we begin with a moment of re-call, bringing forth from our memory the Word of faith. Then we briefly reflect on it and respond to the Reality it bespeaks. We then move to the center, the Presence, in affective love. And finally there abide in contemplation. The four stages are present, and one pre-dominates: contemplation. It is this latter that is seen as the goal when prayer is conceived as a project; we want to get to the stage where contemplation predominates. Or, to express this using an-other, perhaps more classical terminology: one's aim is conceived as getting through the purgative and illuminative stages to the unitive, where we can, in our prayer—and, more and more, outside of it also —retain a sense of our oneness with God, abide in his presence, touch and enjoy him in all persons and things.

Certainly this is a state we do want to enjoy in our lives. And we are realistic in thinking that it is something that will in its full reali-zation come about gradually, something that we can foster by our spiritual practices and especially by serious prayer. But the fallacy I detect here is the tendency to identify particular experiences with certain stages of growth, and in particular to identify a certain kind of prayer, a contemplative type of prayer such as Centering Prayer, with a certain advanced stage of progress, and to make a project of its attainment.

All Christian prayer does imply a certain turning from self to God, some acceptance, however implicit, of his personal revelation of himself, and a response to that. This, therefore, implies some progress. But apart from this basic conversion or turning to God with mind and heart, I do not think we can bind any form of prayer to a particular stage or degree of progress in the Christian or godly life.

I do not mean to deny the validity of the criteria of St. John of the Cross for discerning when one is called to contemplative prayer. But I think his criteria are fulfilled more often than one is led to suspect. Moreover, we have to be aware that his times were very different from our own; we must be attuned to the "signs of the times." With the great shifts that have taken place in our cultures, one is often more open to and stands more in need of the direct experience of God than in times past, when in some of our Christian communities the conceptual approach of God and prayer was more predominant.

William of Saint Thierry wrote a beautiful little treatise *On the Nature and Dignity of Love.* In it he depicts the growth of the Christian, using as his analogue man's natural growth from infancy, through childhood, youth, and maturity to the wisdom of old age. At the conclusion of his very rich and beautiful description, which includes some deeply insightful and loving reflections on our Lord Jesus Christ, William says:

> It must be remembered, however, that the stages of love [we can substitute the word prayer, in each case, as it is but an expression of love] are not like the rungs of a ladder. The soul does not leave the lesser love behind it as it moves onward to the more perfect. All the degrees of love work together as one, and for this reason another soul's experience of the scale of love may well follow an order which differs from the one I have described.

In other words, if we want to think in terms of a ladder, then we should see the ladder lying flat on the ground, so that we can be on all the rungs at the same time.

Growth in the Christian life is a matter of intensification, of growing toward loving God in Christ with one's *whole* mind, *whole* heart, *whole* soul, and *whole* strength. At any moment, mind, heart, soul, and strength should be in play, each in its own intensity. At a particular time, one may be enjoying a deep experience of union with God on one level, thanks to the touch of his grace, while on another level still be struggling with quite naked passions. In a word, one might be enjoying a contemplative type of prayer while still needing and undergoing a process of purgation of purification in regard to certain deviant tendencies, and a process of growth in understanding in regard to some of the basic facets of the divine revelation.

It is false to identify contemplative prayer with a marked state of

Christian perfection or to consider its practitioner as one who has arrived there. A contemplative type of prayer is a way of prayer open to anyone who truly seeks God. And it is the type of prayer experience that will ordinarily best help one to make progress in the Christian life, to be purified and illumined, and to abide more integrally in union with God in and through all. It is, therefore, not something to be worked toward, a goal, but simply a way to be entered into, and experience that can be enjoyed—and struggled with —by all who seek God.

This means, then, that the experience of contemplative prayer is open to development. The initial experience of union with God is not an ultimate experience. The young religious was right to question after his first experiences: Is this all there is to it? And at the moment he was sharing with me, he well knew the answer, for he had been faithful to contemplative prayer through several years and therefore knew it was an evolving experience.

But it is an experience, and an experience that is beyond thought or feeling or emotion. Therefore, we are not really able to capture it in words. It is good; in fact, it is of the substance of our lives. Once we have begun to be really in touch with it, to know it actually, we will say with that superior general: When I miss it, *I miss it*.

The analogy of married love, it seems to me, can best help one to understand and appreciate the contemplative experience. God himself, in the Old Testament, when he wanted to convey to his people the fullness and intensity of his personal love for them, again and again had recourse to the analogy of human lovers. We, following perhaps not a few of the Fathers, tend to shy away from taking this portrayal of God's love for us with any literalness and are quick to spiritualize it, to reduce it to mere imagery. But it is precisely its integralness on an experiential level that makes human love such an apt image and ultimately makes it worthy of being, in the New Testament, elevated to the sacramental order as the sign of Christ's love for us, his Church.

The analogy has a good bit to say to us in regard to experiential prayer.

Those who use the marital act seeking only gratifying experiences rather than holding it as the most integral way of expressing truly human love find it quickly loses its power to satisfy. New techniques, positions, approaches are sought to increase and vary the stimulation, but the long term is inevitably frustration or at best something far short of full human satisfaction. So, too, the one who uses methods of meditation or prayer to have experiences will soon ask, as did the young religious: Is this all there is to contemplation? And soon one will be trying other methods, looking to diverse traditions and teachers. But if one is truly seeking God, if the use of a method of prayer such as Centering Prayer is undertaken to find a way to express one's love and desire for God in a fuller, more integral, freer way, then the method opens not only to a gratifying experience, but allows the experience gradually, and sometimes quickly, to unfold. Newlyweds would greatly deceive themselves and be much disillusioned if they thought their first bungling attempts at making love were all that sex in marriage could be. Rather, as they attain a greater ease and facility with the bodily expression, it can take its proper role as the vehicle for the fullness of their human and sacramental, grace-enlivened love. Then, free from false and exorbitant expectation, the physical experience will reveal its potential to be part of an ever fuller realization of union of love and life. And so, too, the contemplative experience of God, in harmony with the whole growth of Christian life, which it especially fosters and matures, will daily become a fuller, richer experience.

But the qualitative growth of the unexpressible is no less unexpressible. One will only know by the very experience itself and, to some extent, by its overflow into one's life, that this experience is an ever more meaningful and fulfilling expression of one's being.

As a little boy, I used to enjoy, of a summer's evening, to sit on the top step of the porch and just be there. There was something indescribably good about being there. In the background my grandparents sat, silently, on the porch swing, rarely exchanging a word. I realize now that that something that made this an especially good and memorable experience for me was the currents of love that flowed between those two whose understanding and communion had matured through decades. And these currents reached out to enfold me. The man or woman whose love of God has matured through years of intimacy is the one whose presence brings enfolding love. We usually call such a person a saint. But the person himself is usually too much in the current of love and its outreach to notice anything special going on on the outside. In regard to the inner reality he is apt to say with the Prophet Isaiah, "My secret is mine. My secret is mine."

* * *

But many will still be inclined to ask: As we go on in Centering Prayer, won't we be aware of some progress? Won't we have a greater facility? Won't there be fewer thoughts, greater peace, etc.? I think, in actual fact, we can say yes to such questions. Yet I say that with some hesitancy and fear. For as soon as we begin to approach the Prayer with any expectations, in any way seeking something for ourselves, instead of purely and simply seeking God, we undermine the purity of the Prayer and impede our progress.

Undoubtedly as we repeatedly settle into the Prayer we gain a greater facility to do so. As the Prayer grows in meaningfulness for us, a certain eagerness aids our entry into it. As a greater love compels us to seek the Lord more wholeheartedly, we will more readily let go of lesser concerns to turn to the Presence in our depths. Our chosen word will grow in facility to take us to the depths. In fact, at quiet moments when we are initially not thinking of prayer, the word will arise spontaneously and beckon us to enjoy a moment's repose in the center.

With regard to thoughts: Yes, *in general* we might expect *after a time* that they will be less interfering or at least we will be more comfortable in knowing how to deal with them. The basic surface flow of thoughts and images depends largely on our own particular makeup. Some of us will always be more given to thoughts and feelings than others. But as we grow in love and detachment—two of the many fruits of the Prayer—the particular thought will be less apt to get a hold on us and pull us away from the Presence at the center. Experience will teach us more and more to ignore the apparent or real inspirations and brilliant ideas. We will know that they are actually usually half-baked and that they will usually emerge again at some free moment when we will have the leisure to evaluate and use them. As for our little friend the monitor of self-reflection, with the growth of God-centered love and detachment from self and with his just plain being ignored, he will gradually give up—at least to some extent. As the author of *The Cloud of Unknowing* assures us:

> Should some thought go on annoying you, demanding to know what you are doing, answer with this one word alone. If your mind begins to intellectualize over the meaning and connotations of this little word, remind yourself that its value lies in its simplicity. Do this and I assure you these thoughts will vanish. Why? Because you have refused to develop them with arguing. (Ch. 7)

Increasing peace will let us move through life with less tension, and repeated soakings in the Prayer will release the built-up tensions of the past, so there will be less need of thoughts on that score. So, all in all, we should ordinarily, as time goes on, be freer and freer from thoughts, left more to enjoy uninterruptedly the Presence.

In saying all this I have left aside the possibility of an increased activity on the part of God to draw us into a deeper experience of himself through the graces of what some authors have called passive contemplation. The Lord, of course, is always free to take special initiative and, if he wants, to take us so beyond our own center into himself that we can only speak of ecstasy. But until he so takes a hand in things there will always be some mental activity. And we should expect recurring difficult periods as he leads us into deeper and deeper freedom through a more thoroughgoing purification.

At every stage, the rule remains the same: Whenever we become *aware* of anything, we simply let it go by gently returning to the center by the use of our prayer word.

Because the development we are concerned with here is essentially a question of experience, it can, to put it simply, be known only by experience. The Fathers, when speaking of this, repeatedly say—and I must admit it sounds at first hearing a bit snobbish: Those who have experienced this know what I am talking about. And those who have not, pray that you may have the experience, and then you will know.

I have often told people that if before I entered the monastery anyone had ever given me an idea of the pain and sorrow I would encounter in my years as a monk, I would have run fast in the opposite direction, *because* they could never have conveyed to me the experience of love that I would find. Such experience can be gained only in the living. Having that experience, I have never for a day, an hour, or even for a moment regretted having responded to the Lord's most merciful and gracious invitation.

We have to enter into the experience of Centering Prayer and let God reveal himself to us day by day. I entered the monastery and stayed long enough to "taste and see how sweet is the Lord" because I heard *and saw* the witness of those who were willing to share this way with me. So, too, we need to hear the witness and see in the lives of others the fruits of Centering Prayer, to induce us to practice it faithfully until it itself can reveal to us its own meaning. And we in turn need to share what we receive and let the beauty of the Lord's work in our lives shine forth so that others will be attracted to begin and persevere in the practice till they, too, know and can share. "Freely have you received, freely give."

One can, then, rightly expect to make progress in Centering Prayer. But one should not see that progress primarily or try to evaluate it by what happens on the level of thought or feelings during the Prayer. The reduction of thoughts, the feeling of peace, and so forth are truly accidental and no true norm of what is going on. Above all, we need to avoid coming to the Prayer with expectations. For expectations involve seeking something for ourselves, seeking in some way ourselves, and this undermines the very essence of this Prayer, which is essentially a total, pure seeking of God, a total giving over of ourselves to him. Only by a repeated abiding in this prayer of total self-giving will we, bit by bit, die to our false selves and live more freely unto God so that we come to know more and more fully the experience of being, through a union of love, one with our very God.

VIII

A SCHOOL OF COMPASSION

In his Introduction to William Johnston's book *The Mysticism of the Cloud of Unknowing*, Thomas Merton writes:

> . . . mysticism tends to inspire apprehension even in religious minds. Why? Because the mystic must surrender to a power of love that is greater than human and advance toward God in a darkness that goes beyond the light of reason and of human conceptual knowledge. Furthermore, there is no infallible way of guaranteeing the mystic against every mistake: he can never be perfectly sure of any human technique. Only the grace of God can protect him and guide him. In other words, when we speak of mysticism we speak of an area in which man is no longer completely in command of his own life, his own mind, or of his own will. Yet at the same time his surrender is to a God who is "more intimate to him than his own self" (*intimior intimo meo*, in St. Augustine's words) and therefore mysticism precludes real alienation. In mystical union God and man, while remaining no doubt metaphysically distinct, are practically and experientially "one Spirit," in the words of St. Paul (1 Co. 6:17) quoted in this sense by Christian mystics down the centuries. But because there are also other "spirits" and because man does not possess within himself a natural faculty which can by its own power pass final judgment on the transcendent experience taking place within him, a counterfeit mysticism is not only possible but relatively common.

Father Merton here puts his finger on what is a very real concern that we encounter especially when we first come into contact with or begin to experience a type of prayer in which we go beyond thoughts and images.

God, our most loving Father, launched all of creation simply to share the goodness and beauty of his life and love. And he gave us the opportunity to share that goodness and beauty in a divine way. He gave us the power of free choice. Once we have such freedom, we also have the power to fall short—we can choose something less than God. And we have done just that. In choosing lesser things and making them our gods, we become a source of evil not only for ourselves but also for others. And so we have to contend, as St. Paul says, with a law within ourselves that tends to cause us to deviate and to seek ourselves. But if we really turn to God in the depths of our being, we are turning toward the source and so we are reoriented and everything else will come into harmony.

Complete reintegration does not take place immediately, nor does it come about by our own power, but by God's grace. It is usually a slow process. Contemplative prayer, Centering Prayer, is one of the most effective ways to open us to this grace and also to help us cooperate with it.

As Father Merton said, we do not have in our human faculties the power to make an immediate judgment about what is going on in contemplative prayer, because it goes beyond thought and reason. The only way we can make an authentic discernment is by using the norm that our Lord himself gave us: "You know a tree by its fruits" (Mt. 12:33). We can tell that we are moving in the ways of love under the Holy Spirit, the Spirit of Love, by the fruits that are produced in our lives. "By this shall all men know that you are my disciples, that you have love for one another" (Jn. 13:35). Such true love will be accompanied by all the other fruits of the Spirit: by joy, peace, patience, kindness, benignity, gentleness, long-suffering, and chastity (Ga. 5:22–23). These fruits tell us that we are moving in the Spirit of Love. I think all of them can be summed up in one word, and that word is *compassion*. We become compassionate persons who feel with, are with, in a sensitive and sensing presence—with reality, with God, with his creation, with other persons, with our own true selves.

We like to be *with*—to be in harmony with, to be comfortable with, to be in sympathy with. It is a natural inclination. We feel right when we are in sympathy with others. We are comfortable when things are compatible. We want to arrive at harmony and integration. This is what we are seeking in Centering Prayer: to let go of superficial, false, and limiting constructs and be with who we really are and what we really are: creatures, who come forth from God's love, one with the rest of creation, wholly oriented to finding the fullness of life and love in him; and Christians, who have been given the Christ nature, oriented to be, in Christ, with the Spirit, a complete "yes" to the Father.

One of the immediate effects of Centering Prayer, of experiencing our identification with God and with creation and with all other persons, is a very painful sense of our alienation. When we move to the center, we experience how alienated we are. Alienated, in the first place, from ourselves: it is an unfamiliar land into which we move, for we have lived so long in the fabricated land of our false, superficial selves. We have become so accustomed to the land of unlikeness that when we return to our true home in the land of likeness we do not recognize it. And there is cause, if not for uneasiness, certainly at least for awe—for our true self is mysterious. It cannot be defined or readily grasped, like the false self we ourselves have constructed. No, our true self is a participation of the Divine Being. It is an image of God himself. It is a person of immense beauty, held in tenderest and unlimited love. Far different is this true self from the one with which we have so sadly and painfully identified ourselves for so long.

We are put in touch also with other alienations. There is, above all, our alienation from our Source. How much that flows through our lives is in disharmony with the pure currents of love from which we ultimately flow! (Because Centering Prayer puts us into such deep touch with the reality of our sin and sinfulness, it can aptly be used in the penitential service at Mass or at the celebration of the Sacrament of Reconciliation.)

We also experience how alienated we are from others, even those whom, on more superficial levels, we think of as nearest and dearest. We are put in touch with how much in them we do not move along with, affirm, value. And we touch even more sensitive and agonizing realities: the reality of how other humans so intimately one with us in the Source of Life, are exploited, even unto death, so that we can live in the degree of comfort and affluence we enjoy.

Also, we experience our alienation from an exploited creation.

In all these experiences, Centering Prayer can be very painful. This is perhaps why, even though in many respects the experience of this Prayer is so good, many find it difficult to stay with it in fidelity. Yet we want to. It is a process that must be gone through.

On Mount Athos, in one of the centuries-old churches, I was surprised to see a particular fresco that was brilliant in its colors and overwhelmingly attractive in its beauty. I wondered about this, for most of the magnificent wall paintings are hidden beneath deep layers of lampblack and incense smoke—the accumulation of many years. I was told this story: Some curators once came from the mainland. They wished to restore those age-old frescoes. They asked the monks at least to let them demonstrate the possibilities. As the artisans began to apply their restoratives, the darkened images became totally lost as the dirt and grime and soot were brought out. The monks became alarmed and would allow the workers to go no further, thinking all was lost. It was only later, after the curators had gone away, that the film of treated dirt fell away and the ancient picture shone forth in pristine brilliance.

At times, as the work of restoration of the divine image in us proceeds under the hand of the Divine curator during Centering Prayer, we have to have very great faith in him and patiently let layers of muck come to the surface so that they may fall away. In spite of feelings of ambivalence, or the sense that all we are experiencing is a vast confusion of thoughts and feelings and images, more dark than light, we need to be faithful to our daily practice of the Prayer.

It should be a gentle, if persistent, process. This is one of the reasons why we suggest that ordinarily the meditations should be of relatively limited duration—twenty minutes or so—so that not too much will surface at any one time and there will not be too much to cope with. In this Prayer, at the very time we are confronted with our own pitiable mess, we are in touch with the Source of all grace and strength, and we hear his reassuring words: "My grace is sufficient for you" (2 Co. 12:9). We can then go on in confidence and peace.

This painful sense of our sin and alienation is in fact only the converse side of something very beautiful that is being experienced. We experience our alienation from ourselves precisely because we are now getting in touch with our true self, that wondrously beautiful person who images God himself, who is one with the Son of God, who at every moment comes forth from the immense, creative, and generative love of God. And we come to realize our own beauty, lovableness, lovedness.

Psychologists tell us that the human person experiences at birth a primal anxiety, being separated from the womb. In the months that follow, the child identifies wholly with the mother. But after a couple of months the child needs to become autonomous and begin to develop his own personality. In those first months, the child needs to be dependent, but in time he or she needs to break away and develop a sense of himself or he will never walk, talk, and so on. The child needs to experience "I am." With a loving, caring mother the child develops a sense of trust. He can overcome his fear of separation, his anxiety. He can sense the goodness in himself. The mother's love and caring affirm his existence. However, if the mother has not been loving, caring, affirming, the child is anxious, insecure. He cannot step forward but clings to a symbiotic relation with the mother.

As the person grows and goes on through life, in times of great crisis it is natural for him to regress and touch base with this good, trusting self, loved by mother, and find there the courage to go forward and face the crisis. But if the initial experience had been a bad one and the person returns to it, he will find only more anxiety and not have the courage to step forward. Sad to say, in our times there are perhaps more and more persons who have not had a good initial experience of affirming maternal love and care. It is here where the experience we have in Centering Prayer can have a wonderful healing quality.

In Centering Prayer one regresses, we might say, back beyond even that initial experience with mother, to the deeper, more primal (excuse the expression) and more constant experience of being loved, cared for, and affirmed by the ever active and present creative love of God, Father and Mother. Freud has criticized religious experience as being a regressive return to the womb, creating a symbiotic relation with a mother-God, a mother who will provide all, and leading to an oceanic feeling of oneness with God and all life. There is some truth in Freud's analysis, yet his interpretation is wrong. For one who with faith experiences the living God, experiences life directly in "I am," comes to know his true self, and then is able to relate with God and others as others in a response of love.

Such a regression is healthy and healing; it is life-engendering. For those who have never had a good grounding experience of caring love, the experience of God in contemplative prayer can be the ground for a wholly new kind of life, giving them the courage to step forward into loving, creative, and satisfying modes of activity. For everyone, to step back periodically and experience such grounding cannot but have a powerful influence on the way he or she relates to self, to God, to others, to all life's activity.

How affirming! At every moment, God himself attends to us in love, sharing with us his being and his life. How freeing! For in him we form a new self-identification—one not dependent on accidentals, differences, specialties, like being a doctor, lawyer, monk, biologist who stands out among his fellows because he does or has some special thing. An identity based on differentiation (and how many of us do spontaneously seek to identify and introduce ourselves according to our professions and accomplishments) is a fragile one indeed, and leaves us fearful and defensive. What if someone else does what I do—my identity is lost! Far from it. Being in touch with our true selves we form a new self-identity, one that flows from what is essential. I am a human person, the image of God; I am a Christian, one with the Son of God, another Christ. This is a shared identity, one that lies in the full affirmation of sameness. There is no fragility here. There is strength in unity.

There is no room left for competition. There are thankfulness and joy. Thomas Merton touched upon this experience when he wrote in his journal:

> Thank God, thank God, that I *am* like other men, that I am only a man among others. . . . It is a glorious distinction to be a member of the human race.

Most of us have to struggle with a very poor self-image—sometimes more, sometimes less. Negative attitudes toward ourselves have been programmed into us by negative feedback from parents, teachers, and others all along the course of our lives. In many cases, we have tried to hide this even from ourselves by the false self-image we have constructed—that fragile thing that calls for so much defensive care. In other cases we let the negativity dominate much of our sense of self.

When we can realize that all such judgments are being made in the light of false norms, false evaluations of what truly constitutes our worth as human persons, we can let those negative judgments and feelings go. When we experience our true beauty and worth in God's creative and adoptive love, the negativity we are tempted to feel about ourselves melts away and gives place to joy and freedom. Secure in our own true worth, we no longer need to be competitive or jealous or stand on the head of the other to bolster our slumping ego. We can stand in the crowd and not be lost, because we know we are uniquely the object of a divine Love.

And we will want to stand in the crowd. That is another effect of Centering Prayer. As Merton said, we rejoice in our oneness with all, because that is the reality—the reality we come to truly experience in Centering Prayer. At the center, at the Source of our being, we find all others—for our Source is also their Source. We find that all others are one with us in coming forth from creative love, one with us in the call to be one with the Son. Out of this oneness flow love and care and communion. Merton said in *New Seeds of Contemplation:* "When you and I become what we are really meant to be, we will discover not only that we love one another perfectly but that we are both living in Christ and Christ in us and we are all one Christ. We will see that it is he who loves in us." (p. 65)

We can now perceive how all the fruits of the Holy Spirit flow out of the experience of Centering Prayer. Love—I sense deeply my oneness with everyone else and their beauty and my beauty in God. What else can there be but a communion of love?

And joy—not only in my own being, but in everyone else's. I can rejoice in the goodness and beauty of others because they are no longer a threat to me. There is no longer any room for competition. Their good is my good because we are one.

St. Bernard of Clairvaux, one of the first great abbots of the Cistercian Order, is famous, among other things, for his treatise called the *Apologia*. It was written in connection with the controversy that developed between the newly reformed Cistercians and the monks who continued to follow the usages of the previous century, commonly called the Black Monks. In his masterful work, Bernard first praises the Black Monks; then he takes to task his own confreres who are attacking them; and in a final, better-known section, he denounces with consummate satire the abuses prevailing among the unreformed. In the course of the first section he sounds a note of warning that contains a very valuable insight. He says to the Black Monks: "Beware! All the beauty that you possess as part of your tradition might belong more to me than to you, for it does in fact belong most to the one who loves it most."

Bernard's spiritual son, St. Aelred of Rievaulx, abbot of a monastery in Yorkshire, proclaims the same reality in a sermon to his monks on the feast of the Assumption. He recounts a vision he experienced after the long, solemn, and rich vigil they had celebrated in the church that night. In this vision the Lord made it clear to him that all the beauty and merit of the great Office belonged more to a lay brother out on the hill watching the sheep than to any monk in choir, because the brother loved it more.

This is the realization behind Pope Pius XI's proclamation of St. Thérèse of Lisieux as the greatest missionary of modern times. Thérèse loved the work of the missionaries even more than did the missionaries themselves.

When we get in touch with the solidarity we have in Christ, in God, in our common humanness, there is no room left for competition. Rather, only affirmation. For all the beauty, goodness, and activity of each member are ours and to our merit, to the extent to which we make them ours by choosing them in love. What a boon this is for ecumenism, in relating with non-Christian religions and in our dialogue with Marxism and with the secular world. When this realization begins to flow not only out of a conviction in faith but out of an experience of the reality, then it is effectively present in our life not only at times by reflective act but constantly by connatural response. "All things are yours and you are Christ's and Christ is God's" (1 Co. 3:22–23). All good things are ours, with all their goodness and beauty, and so our lives are grounded in constant joy.

This does not mean that we do not suffer. If we become truly compassionate persons, more in touch with ourselves and others and the oneness that exists among us all, we are going to suffer more than we ever did before, but it is going to be a suffering that has at its heart a deep joy. It is something of the suffering of a mother at the crib of her sick child. She would not give up her share in her child's suffering for anything in the world. Try to tell her to go away and forget about it . . . that we will take care of the child. Oh, no! Her whole being, her whole joy, is to be there with her child. Such suffering reflects something of the suffering of Christ on the cross and is a participation in it. On the cross at the very moment that he was crying: "My God, my God, why have you forsaken me?" he was enjoying a deep union with the Father in perfect love, and probably even the beatific vision. It is difficult to put that together! Yet it is certainly something that we do come to experience! A joy in our union with God and with all our brothers and sisters and in being with them in their sufferings.

Out of such experience necessarily flow kindness, patience, longsuffering, benignity. When we sense our oneness with others, when we are filled with compassion, how can we not be kind, patient, benign? And chaste, too? As we sense our own beauty and goodness, we are impelled to have reverence and respect for our own bodies and thus for the bodies of others, the exquisite works of God's constantly present creative love.

Then there is peace—that peace that flows from being in harmony with our true selves, with our God, with all others, with the whole of creation. Peace is the tranquillity of order.

Father Dominique-Georges Pire, winner of the Nobel Peace Prize, wrote: "I still think that to be a peacemaker—that is to say, a man of peace—one must first be at peace with oneself. One must first achieve inner peace. This involves getting to know oneself. . . . Only then can a peaceful being approach the immense task of creating harmony between groups and between individuals." Merton would certainly agree with Father Pire.

When we are in touch with the Source of Being, we find there not only ourselves and all other persons coming forth from Creative Love, but also the whole of creation; we realize our solidarity with all creatures and hold them in reverence. I am convinced that this experience, with its consequent reverence, is the only possible basis for a true and complete ecology. Only when a true reverence pervades our every contact with the created, will our use of them be what it should be.

Such a realization can descend to very practical details in our everyday life. For example: coming into a true reverence for God's gift of food, we realize and respect the fact that its purpose is to nourish us and to bind us together in communion and sharing. To overeat, then, or to eat improperly, to abuse food, is sacrilegious. It is a disreverence for something that shares in the divine goodness and has a place in the divine plan.

Some years ago, shortly after the inauguration of Cistercian Publications, we had the joy of publishing a *Festschrift* in honor of Dr. Jeremiah F. O'Sullivan, the father of Cistercian studies in America. Dr. O'Sullivan was an immensely loved professor who had a very great impact on his students. This was reflected in the fact that so many of them followed him into the field of Cistercian studies. In the course of the presentation luncheon, someone asked the guest of honor to what he attributed his success. This very learned and rather sophisticated university professor, a happily married man, gave a very moving, profound, and yet simple answer: "I saw the image of God in each of my students, and I worshiped." Jerry's reverence did not stop there. In his back yard in Trenton he raised some of the largest and most magnificent vegetables I have ever seen outside of Mount Athos. I am told that, each morning, Jerry would go out among them and talk and even sing to them as he gently and lovingly tended them. He certainly did not let that bit of earth lie fallow.

Merton once wrote: "The discovery of the 'true self' is also a discovery of one's responsibility to other such selves, one's brothers in Christ, one's fellow men." I would add: ". . . and women and the whole of the creation." And Merton was certainly aware of this. He wrote, in *Contemplation and a World of Action:*

> The world as pure object is something that is not there. It is not a reality outside us. . . . It is a living, self-creating mystery of which I myself am a part, to which I am myself my own unique door. When I find the world in my own ground, it is impossible for me to be alienated by it.

In his *Dialogues,* Pope St. Gregory the Great sought to give us insight into the spirit that made St. Benedict of Nursia the worthy father of the monks of the West. In a culminating scene, St. Gregory describes a vision St. Benedict enjoyed one night as he stood at his window in prayer. Suddenly he beheld the whole of creation, contained as it were in one ray of light. In this account, I think the great Pastoral Pope was seeking by image to indicate the fruit of the holy monk's prayer. In the light or the darkness of contemplative prayer, all comes together.

Once we have had this experience in contemplative prayer, there is no dichotomy between work and prayer. All work becomes prayer. For, by a connatural sensitivity to God's creative presence in each and every person, thing, and action, we perceive and reverence God and respond to him in love in all that we see and do. In each person we encounter, we see the Lord and the person's beauty in the Lord, and we respond and reverence and love. In each of our own movements and activities, we perceive God's active presence at the source of the energy we use, and our hearts move simultaneously in gratitude and love. In each thing we use, we are aware of the creative Presence, which is each moment bringing it forth, and we worship.

I am sure most of us have had the experience at one time or another of the crushing weight of compassion. Before I became a monk, I did some work in Brooklyn in the Bedford-Stuyvesant area. It was before drugs had invaded the scene, so the situation was not as bad as it would later become. Yet we averaged a murder a night in the parish. I would work in the afternoon with the Confraternity of Christian Doctrine and C.Y.O. programs. When evening came, I would lock the church and then prostrate before the Blessed Sacrament and let the pain seep out. What could we do to begin to respond to the need that surrounded us on every side? I felt I was going to be torn to pieces, to be completely consumed in trying to respond to each one.

But it is a very different experience when compassion grows in us through contemplative prayer. At the very time this heightened sensitivity of oneness with others is making its demands upon us, we also experience within us the Spirit of God, and so we have the wherewithal to peacefully respond to each one. We do not have to depend on our own littleness or emptiness; we have all the power of the love of God. I know there was a tremendous difference in my experience when I traveled in Boston and New York before I had gotten in touch with this reality and after. It used to be a very draining experience, and it got worse and worse as I became more and more sensitive. I would sit in a bus with sixty people and look at their faces and feel torn to pieces. I wanted to take each one in my arms and try to respond in some way to all that I sensed there, all that was being expressed by their body language, their faces, the patent message of their terrible need and loneliness. But when I began to sense the intimate presence of God, I was able to touch them, love them, embrace them in him. And I could sense the healing that was taking place. The Presence was there. God was pouring forth his fullness, his healing love.

When we begin to realize that the Spirit of Love is in us as our Spirit, we can begin to really love according to the command of the New Law, which is not to love as we would love but as Jesus loves. Jesus said: "I give you a new commandment. You are to love as I have loved you." When we experience the Presence and the Power of Love, we can pour out our life as Christ did on the cross when his side was opened and blood and water poured forth, pouring out upon the Church the fullness of the Holy Spirit of Love.

Perceiving the intrinsic goodness of all that is does not mean, however, that we become blind to the fact of evil, to the absence of due good and order. Christ was well aware of it. His whip struck out within the very precincts of his Father's house. Even that partial and prevailing lack of goodness that we call lukewarmness filled him with disgust (Rv. 3). Yet we are called to be perfect even as our heavenly Father is perfect, who lets his rain fall on the good and the bad alike. We are to bring reverence and love to all. And if we can be in touch with the deeper presence of goodness even in the worst of those we must live and work with and for, we will more easily, as well as more adequately, fulfill the legitimate demands of the Gospel.

I am always a little fearful, when I speak about or discuss the effects of Centering Prayer, that, no matter what I say, we may be seduced into looking for some results within the Prayer itself. During the Prayer, we must not concern ourselves with how we pray or what is happening or anything else. We must center our attention on God himself, truly present. And each time we are drawn to anything else, we must return simply, gently, to the Lord with our word. This is one thing I would like to underline about eighteen times. We cannot judge this Prayer in itself and we must not try to. The fruits of Centering Prayer are to be perceived and experienced outside the time of the Prayer itself and are the sure sign of the presence and work of the Spirit of Love within our refreshing work of love.

When a pond is greatly agitated by the breezes and the wind, one can throw in a pebble or even many pebbles and there is no noticeable effect. When a pond is perfectly at peace and one casts a pebble into it, the gentle waves spread in every direction till they reach even the farthest shore. When we are in the midst of a busy everyday life, so many thoughts go in and out of our minds and our hearts, we do not perceive the effect they are having upon us. But when we come to achieve a deeper inner quiet, then we are much more discerning. The way is open to follow even the most gentle leadings of the Spirit and to avoid even the most subtle deviations that are suggested either by the self or by the evil one. By Centering Prayer, with the help of the Holy Spirit, we can hope to establish this deep inner quiet, so that even in the midst of everyday activities, this lively sensitivity will remain and all our activities will be guided by the call of grace and the leading of the Holy Spirit.

Last Christmas, my mother gave me an amaryllis. I was absolutely delighted as I watched this plant grow. Growing things always fascinate me, and the new life sprang out of the dormant bulb so rapidly that it was particularly exciting. Just before bursting into bloom, and giving us the gift of beauty, odor, and delight, the outer leaves of the bud took the form of two hands folded in prayer. In this has the Lord given us another sacrament. A life of activity that is first enfolded in prayer, in which each activity comes forth out of prayer, is a life that is going to be immensely beautiful, a life that gives forth a good odor, a life that is a delight to all who come into contact with it. The author of *The Cloud of Unknowing* speaks of persons who have become even physically attractive, beautiful, through the practice of contemplative prayer. I have seen such persons and I hope you have too. May we, too, by God's mercy become such persons.

In Centering Prayer we do not seek ourselves, we do not seek anything for ourselves. We seek the living God. But in finding him, we find all things besides: My God and my All.

IX

KEEPING THE LIGHT OF TABOR

Some years ago, I had the grace-filled privilege of spending some time in the Holy Land. Day after day, Bible in hand, I trod the roads that once knew the footsteps of the Master, his disciples, his Mother, the multitude of prophetic witnesses that went before, the first "Christians" who came after. Many of the hallowed places touched me deeply—Elijah's cave before Haifa, David's tomb near the Cenacle, the crypt of the Virgin by Gethsemani, the pavement of the Pretorium, the empty burial vault, and nearby Calvary—and each had its own particular message as I stood or sat or knelt there, reading again the familiar Scriptures as if I had never read or heard them before. It was a deepening experience.

But of all the sites that I touched or that touched me, none so etched itself and its mystic meaning on my soul as that of the quiet, peaceful summit that rises over the Sea of Galilee and still seems in some mysterious way to retain the penumbra of that Light that once bespoke the fullness of the Divine Presence. The fact that tourist buses cannot navigate the tortuous ascent undoubtedly contributes to the peace on Tabor's height. But what one finds there, or at least what I found, was something far more deep and transcendent than that mode of quiet.

Undoubtedly the monk's particular attraction to the mystery of the Transfiguration had something to do with my experience. In some sense, this event seems almost to transcend that of the holy

Easter event. On Tabor we are given a glimpse of the reality that Easter speaks of: the glory of the Risen Christ, the consummation of human dignity and exaltation. And monks are the ones who, like Peter, babble, "Let us build cells here." But, unlike Peter, they receive the divine assent and are invited to abide in the Cloud of Divine Light.

This mystery, this saving event of Transfiguration, says much about the reality of the Centering Prayer experience. Let us listen again to St. Mark's account:

> Six days later, Jesus took with him Peter and James and John and led them up a high mountain where they could be alone by themselves. There in their presence he was transfigured: his clothes became dazzlingly white, whiter than any earthly bleacher could make them. Elijah appeared to them with Moses; and they were talking with Jesus. Then Peter spoke to Jesus: "Rabbi," he said, "it is wonderful for us to be here; so let us make three tents, one for you, one for Moses and one for Elijah." He did not know what to say; they were so frightened. And a cloud came, covering them in shadow; and there came a voice from the cloud, "This is my Son, the Beloved. Listen to him." Then suddenly, when they looked round, they saw no one with them any more but only Jesus (9:2–8).

To enter into the experience of Tabor the three disciples had to accept the invitation to go apart for a while, to leave the plain of everyday cares and doings and follow the beckoning of the Lord to come with him to a rendezvous with the Father. It was mysterious. There seemed to be nothing in the place where they were going. They had only their faith in the Lord Jesus and their love for him to guide them up the mountain.

So it is as we sit down to center. We must move on in faith and love. We must leave behind all the cares and concerns, the images of the plain, and all we can understand. We seem to be headed into nothingness, and many times that seems to be as far as we get—we are still on the journey. But if we persevere, the summit, the center, will be attained, and then. . . .

The Lord had led the three into this solitude in order to pray, and "as he prayed his visage was changed and his clothing became brilliant as lightning." If we persevere in this prayer, the enlightening will come. And not only will we come to see the Lord in his glory, but we will even be enveloped in the glory of the Divine, the Taboric, Light, and have impressed upon us the very words, or, rather, the fullness of the Word of the Father. We will come to know that the essence of prayer, of all Christian life, is that total response of receptive listening.

But in the transcendent scene, we find the seemingly curious presence of Moses and Elijah, and they, too, are speaking. Moses is the figure of the Law, Elijah, of the Prophets. Together they sum up the Scriptures, the Revelation that led up to, summoned us to the Revelation that is the *central* figure of the tableau and of all our lives, the Transfigured Christ, mediator of the Cloud of the Divine Light. We are reminded that it is ordinarily through the receptive reading of the Sacred Scripture that we are invited, summoned to seek the Lord in faith and love, the first movement of Centering Prayer.

Lectio is very important in the life of one who centers. It is this meeting with the Lord in his revealed word that motivates us to seek him at the center. Conversely, the experience of God in the center, the cloud of unknowing, awakens in us a desire to know him more intimately, to seek him and knowledge about him in the Revelation. It is a self-enlivening cycle.

This experience of God at the center of our being also creates in us a desire to stay there enjoying the holy and wholly satisfying presence: "Lord, it is good for us to be here. Let us build tents." We want to stay. And, as I mentioned, this is the contemplative's vocation, to be able to pitch his or her tent and stay. Others must descend again with the Lord—for he is where his will is—to the plain, and sustained by the pervading presence-making memory of the vision, to which they will regularly return, they will pursue their ministry and fill up what is wanting in the Passion of Christ.

As the experience of the vision drew to a close, the disciples, after being overwhelmed by the cloud of unknowing, saw only Jesus. This is indeed the fruit of Centering Prayer. We begin to see "only Jesus." Jesus, indeed, is perceived more and more as *the* center of our lives and existence. And we begin to see in all and everything, at the center, only Jesus in his creative and re-creating love. "Only Jesus" gives things, events, persons, life, and existence itself their meaning. We truly become Christians. We know that "all things are ours and we are Christ's and Christ is God's." We are truly centered.

As the disciples descended with Jesus from the saving event, they were warned "to tell no one what they had seen, until after the Son of Man had risen from the dead." But now the Son of Man is risen, and we should proclaim to all what we have seen and experienced at the center and how they, too, can heed the Lord's invitation, "Come apart for a while. . . ." "Be still, and *know* that I am God." It is time to share, to proclaim, to teach.

Reflecting on the Transfiguration brings to my mind an experience I had in a Centering Prayer workshop some years ago. I was having the great joy on that particular occasion of sharing with the faculty of the seminary of my home diocese. As was my wont, on the last evening of the workshop I invited the participants to evaluate our days together. At this point one of the young priests made a poignant plea. The workshop had been for him a great experience—a Taboric experience, he said. He had had such experiences before in the course of retreats, though never so full and satisfying. But, in times past, after he had descended to the plain, in a week or two or three, the light began to fade. He did not want that to happen this time. What could he do?

I took that question home with me that night and held it in concerned prayer. In the morning, I returned to the group with a simple exercise for formulating a rule of life, which I have described in the Epilogue of *Daily We Touch Him*. It might be worthwhile repeating it here, with a certain elaboration.

In undertaking to formulate a rule of life for ourselves, the first and most important thing we must do is get in touch as fully and deeply as we can with our true selves and with all the levels of our being. We need to reflect on those words of St. Paul to the Corinthians that we read in the first chapter of this book: ". . . the depths of God can be known only by the Spirit of God." We are partakers of the divine nature. We have been baptized into the Son of God. We are one with Christ. It is, then, only the Holy Spirit who knows the depths of our being. We must, if we hope to formulate a rule of life that corresponds to who we truly are, call upon the Holy Spirit for help and rely on him.

In the Prologue of his Holy Rule, St. Benedict tells his disciples that whenever they begin any undertaking they must call upon God with most insistent prayer. That is most truly our need here. We would do well to reflect again on that passage from First Corinthians and then spend some time in silent, searching prayer before we begin to elaborate our rule.

After this prayer and reflection, we are ready to begin the labor—and it is a bit of a labor—to elaborate our own personal rule of life. I would encourage you to do this with pencil in hand, writing out each section on a separate sheet of paper as you work with it. We should take lots of time, not rush it in any way. We need time to listen to the Spirit, to listen to ourselves. If this is done in the right spirit, it is truly a time of prayer. It can prove to be a real retreat—a stepping back to take cognizance of our forces in order to step forward to a fuller and more vital attack on life and eternal life: The Kingdom of Heaven suffers violence and only the violent will carry it away.

The first step is to try to get in touch with what we really want out of life, what we really want to do with our life. We have to be very realistic here.

I once knew a little girl who cried for the moon. Whenever there was a full moon, she would stand in her crib, clutching the bars, and cry and cry, because she wanted that big bright moon and no one would let her have it. You might say she was a "lunatic." But there is apt to be a bit of the lunatic in all of us, reaching for things that are beyond us and thus causing ourselves endless frustration.

On the other hand, we must not sell ourselves short. I think this is the most common failure: we expect too little of God and we expect too little of ourselves. We must seek what will really fulfill us as human persons, as Christian men and women. Much of the unhappiness in our world comes from our seeking to find fulfillment and happiness in things that ultimately cannot satisfy us. In fact, only One can truly satisfy us, and that is our God: "We are made for you, O Lord, and our souls will not rest until they rest in you."

To choose as the ultimate goal of our lives anything less than God will leave us frustrated, unsatisfied, despairing of finding any meaning that is worthy of us, anything that can satisfy the limitless hunger of our minds to know, of our hearts to love. If we do not see all the other things we choose in life as in some way opening out to this infinite fullness, they will prove to be dead ends. No matter how good and beautiful they may be, no matter how much of ourselves we invest in them, there will come a time when we will say: "Is this all there is?" And life will appear as a cruel joke, a project that can only lead to frustration and misery. It will be something we need to escape from by drugs, liquor, the passing excitement of sex; something we will try to sleep off or let slip away while we sit mindless before the "boob tube." For only so long can we chase, breathless, after passing goods before we discover the cruelty of their limits.

But even as we choose the Infinite, we realize the almost infinite number of options our good Father has left open to us as ways to grow and respond to Infinite Life and Love. As we consult our own gifts, talents, and actual opportunities, our perimeters are narrowed: as a human person, as a Christian, as one with a particular chosen vocation, what do I want to do? What do I want to pursue? We want to formulate as clearly and as concisely as we can, just what we want to do, want to have, seeing as clearly as possible how each thing we choose contributes, plays its part in bringing us to our ultimate goal, the fullest and deepest possible union with our God of love.

Once we have formulated our goals or aims in life, we move on to the second step. Here we want to list as fully as we can all that we need to do and to have in order to attain these goals. Again, we need to be very realistic and to consider every level of ourselves. As a man or woman, a human person of body and soul, I need a certain amount of food and rest, work and recreation, friendship and solitude. As a Christian, I need to pray, to hear the Word of God, and to be nourished by the sacraments. I need the support of the Christian community. In my chosen vocation, I need certain knowledge, certain tools, et cetera. I take inventory of all these things, and, yes, the virtues I need, the self-discipline to use them properly.

Seeing what I need, I am ready to move on to the third step. Here I stand still for a moment and jut a glance over my shoulder to the past. Perhaps I can look over the past six months, or the time reaching back to a significant event that charted my recent life and activity: marriage, a retreat, graduation, religious profession. . . . As I survey the intervening scene, I ask myself: What, during this period of time, has been preventing me from doing what I really want to do? From being who I really want to be? What things within myself, in my activities, in my life situation, in the activity and attitudes of those who touch my life, have been obstacles to growth, to moving ahead on my chosen path?

As I mentioned before, it is well as we move through this exercise to take plenty of time, to depend very much on the Holy Spirit, and to write things down as we see them.

With the fruit of these three points of reflection before us, we are now ready to move to the fourth and perhaps the most difficult part of this work. Seeing what we really want and what we have to do to get it, to be it, and what has been keeping us from it, we are now ready to begin to formulate a practical program for ourselves that will provide time and space to do those things we need to do to get what we want out of life. What we need each day: so much sleep, food, prayer, sacred reading, work, recreation, et cetera. We may even want and find it helpful to program quite precisely: rise at such a time, exercise for so long, meditate at such times, breakfast at seven o'clock, and so forth. There will be other elements to program on a weekly basis, others on a monthly basis.

One thing I think is very important: a monthly day, or at least half day, of recollection. This is the time when we again sit down with our rule of life and see how things are going. This can be a moment of great satisfaction. We can look back over the past month and see that, overall, our life has been moving in the direction we want it to move; that we are truly in command of ourselves and our destiny.

A word of caution here: a rule of life is not so much a thing to be lived as a thing to be lived out of. It gives us a supportive structure. Life is a very variable thing. It is life, and it goes in all directions. To return again to the image of the trellis that supports the climbing rose: the luxuriant vine, full of life, reaches out in every direction as it climbs upward, but it keeps coming back to find support on the mounting rungs of the trellis. If the rungs were not there, the vine would fall back on itself and fail to mount higher in its reach for ever fuller life and vitality in the sun. Our rule is there. Some days, the swift current of life carries us in many directions. We miss sleep and meditation and meals and our exercises. But as the flow slows down again, we fall back upon our rule and move ahead with its support. It channels our energies in the direction we want to go, like the sturdy banks of a watercourse.

Frequently, as we review our rule of life on our monthly retreat day, we will see where it is not really corresponding to our evolving life situation. We should have no hesitation about reforming it. It is there in service of life. As we grow, our vision expands and our situation changes. Various elements take on greater or lesser significance. We will probably come to need less sleep and less food as our life becomes more satisfying and more relaxed and energized by regular meditation. At one time, we will need more study, reading, reflection, and prayer; at another, more sharing and activity to bring the fruit of our study into life-giving reality.

This fourth step—the actual formulation of a rule of life—can indeed be the most difficult. For it is here that we actually establish our hierarchy of values and make our choices. God our Father, in his great love, has endowed us with so much and lays before us so many options that we cannot possibly pursue them all. And yet they are all so good. It is difficult enough to lay aside the evil, but to lay aside the truly good. . . . But it is precisely herein that the value of a rule of life lies, especially for good and generous persons. So often do we frustrate ourselves by pursuing so many goods that we make scant progress in any of them. In this we are in danger of becoming discouraged, despairing of attaining any good, and abandoning all. We need to courageously make choices, opt for a reasonable number of goods, and resolutely let others go, so that the chosen ones can truly blossom in our lives. Such choice is difficult. To live it out consistently is more difficult. To experience the fruit of it is most wonderful.

In the Gospel of St. Luke there is a curious parable:

"And indeed, which of you here, intending to build a tower, would not first sit down and work out the cost to see if he had enough to complete it? Otherwise, if he laid the foundation and then found himself unable to finish the work, the onlookers would all start making fun of him and say, 'Here is a man who started to build and was unable to finish.' Or again, what king marching to war against another king would not first sit down and consider whether with ten thousand men he could stand up to the other who advanced against him with twenty thousand? If not, then while the other king was still a long way off, he would send envoys to sue for peace. So in the same way none of you can be my disciple unless he gives up all his possessions" (14:28–33).

I am sure we have read this passage or heard it read many times. But I wonder if you have ever reflected on it. The words that are very striking to me are: "So in the same way." Now, how is what follows the same as that which goes before? How is "none of you can be my disciple unless he gives up all his possessions" the same as a man who sits down and figures out if he has enough money to build a house or fight a war? What is our Lord saying to us in this parallel? Just what we have been talking about: If we want to be his disciples, we have to follow Christ and follow him as our Master. And we have to give up everything to do this. He gave up everything. In another place our Lord spells this out: father, mother, sister, brother, home, family, and even our very selves. All things have to be given up as being goals in themselves in order that we might be to God. Now, how does this tie in with planning to build a house or fight a war?

We don't give up everything just by a single decision or wish. We sometimes get the idea that when our Lord talks about our becoming disciples it means we just drop everything and follow him. The apostles went back to their fishnets and familiar surroundings again and again after their initial call. Even after the resurrection, our Lord found them fishing. Because the giving up includes giving up self, giving up all our attachments, as well as our family and our friends, our investments and material goods, it does not happen in a moment. It is something that takes time. And the question is, are we going to be able to carry through? Or are we going to get stuck in the foundations?

As our Lord was saying: some get just so far and then are not able to carry through. So we have to sit down and make a plan. I think that is precisely what the Lord is saying to us here: If you want to be my disciple, you have to sit down and figure out concretely how you are going to organize your forces and carry through to completion what you really want to do. How are we going to win our battle against all the forces against us, the forces in society, in our own homes and communities, in our own inclinations and habits, in all the demands that are put on us and that we can put on ourselves? These are concrete questions and we have to sit down and figure them out. How are we going to build a tower—or is it a trellis to support life? This is precisely what is involved in putting together a rule of life.

If the meaning of our life, of our whole existence, is to love and to develop a relationship with God, then we need prayer more than we need food or sleep or anything else. It is essential if we are going to function in a reasonable way as humans in human society. We have to have prayer in our daily lives. It is a demand of our very nature, of our very being; it is something that has to be there. We can skip a meal much easier than we can skip prayer. If we are really in touch with ourselves, we will realize it is not only something we need—it is something we want. It satisfies our deepest longings and desires.

And it is something God really wants too. This is sometimes difficult for us to understand and accept: that God really wants our love, our attention, our time.

In the prophecy of Ezekiel, the Lord gives the prophet a very graphic message for the people:

> "The Lord Yahweh says this: By origin and birth you belong to the land of Canaan. Your father was an Amorite and your mother a Hittite. At birth, the very day you were born, there was no one to cut your navel string or wash you in cleansing water, or rub you with salt, or wrap you in napkins. No one leaned kindly over you to do

anything like that for you. You were exposed in the open fields; you were as unloved as that on the day you were born.

"I saw you struggling in your blood as I was passing, and I said to you as you lay in your blood: Live, and grow like the grass of the fields. You developed, you grew, you reached marriageable age. Your breasts and your hair both grew, but you were quite naked. Then I saw you as I was passing. Your time had come, the time for love. I spread part of my cloak over you and covered your nakedness; I bound myself by oath, I made a covenant with you—it is the Lord Yahweh who speaks—and you became mine. I bathed you in water, I washed the blood off you, I anointed you with oil. I gave you embroidered dresses, fine leather shoes, a linen headband and a cloak of silk. I loaded you with jewels, gave you bracelets for your wrists and a necklace for your throat. I gave you nose ring and ear-rings; I put a beautiful diadem on your head. . . . The fame of your beauty spread through the nations, since it was perfect, be-cause I had clothed you with my own splendor—it is the Lord Yah-weh who speaks.

"You have become infatuated with your own beauty; you have used your fame to make yourself a prostitute; you have offered your services to all comers. . . . You have taken your clothes to brighten your high places and there you have played the whore. . . . You have taken my presents of gold and silver jewelry and made your-self human images to use in your whorings. You have taken your embroidered clothes and put them on the images, and the oil and incense which are rightly mine you have offered to them. The bread I gave you, the finest flour, oil and honey with which I used to feed you, you have now offered to them as an appeasing fragrance. . . .

"For the Lord Yahweh says this: I will treat you as you deserve, you who have despised your oath even to the extent of breaking a covenant, but I will remember the covenant that I made with you when you were a girl, and I will conclude a covenant with you that shall last for ever. . . . I am going to renew my covenant with you; and you will learn that I am Yahweh, and so remember and be cov-ered with shame, and in your confusion be reduced to silence, when I have pardoned you for all that you have done—it is the Lord Yah-weh who speaks." (Ch. 16)

Our basic human misery could hardly be depicted more poignantly, nor the lavish goodness of our God; our overwhelming ingratitude in misusing his gifts and his unending fidelity stand in sharpest contrast. He uses marital imagery to indicate the intimacy and the passion of his desire for us. No matter what misery we have arisen from, no matter how unfaithful we have been, how abusive of his goodness, he still wants our love, wants to be intimate with us. This is a word he speaks powerfully again and again in his self-revelation. In the prophet Osee he shows himself a foolish lover, marrying a harlot and again and again pursuing her and bringing her back after her repeated infidelities. In the Book of Revelation he clearly expresses his disgust with our lukewarmness, yet shows himself standing tirelessly at the door of our hearts, knocking, waiting for us to open and let him in. God really wants—*needs* because he wants—our love, our attention, our time, our prayer. Our failure to grasp this, to believe that our prayer is important to our Lord, undermines our fidelity to prayer. If we really believe it is important, important to God, it will be important to us, too.

In the opening verses of the twelfth chapter of St. John's Gospel we have an important word. We can tell it is a word that the early Christian community discerned as important, for it is found both in the Synoptics and in St. John. Moreover, they not only situate it in an important place in their narratives—immediately before the ultimate account of the Paschal Mystery—but in introducing it John insists on the presence of the risen Lazarus, Jesus' greatest miracle prior to and foreshadowing the crowning event of his own resurrection. Let us listen to this word:

> Six days before the Passover, Jesus went to Bethany, where Lazarus was, whom he had raised from the dead. They gave a dinner for him there; Martha waited on them and Lazarus was among those at table. Mary brought in a pound of very costly ointment, pure nard, and with it anointed the feet of Jesus, wiping them with her hair. The house was full of the scent of the ointment. Then Judas Iscariot—one of his disciples, the man who was to betray him —said, "Why wasn't this ointment sold for three hundred denarii, and the money given to the poor?" . . . Jesus said, "Leave her

alone; she had to keep this scent for the day of my burial. You have the poor with you always, you will not always have me" (Jn. 12:1-8).

Mark adds these words of our Lord:

"I tell you solemnly, wherever throughout all the world the Good News is proclaimed, what she has done will be told also, in remembrance of her" (Mk. 14:9).

For once, we are almost tempted to be in sympathy with Judas, thief and traitor though he be. Here is this woman with this fabulously expensive jar of perfume. Three hundred denarii—that is, three hundred days' wages; by today's standards, thousands of dollars. The very best and most exotic of perfumes, in an exquisite alabaster jar—Paris could hardly match it today. And, as one of the Synoptics brings out, Mary did not simply open the jar and pour out a few powerful drops, nor did she content herself with pouring out the whole of the contents. She broke the precious jar and let the whole of its richness gush out. What extravagance! With Judas, something in us cries: What waste! And yet she is not only defended by the Master, she is praised and exalted. The good fragrance fills the whole house. What she has done benefits the whole Church. And wherever the Good News is proclaimed, this is to be an integral part of it, an integral part of Christian life. Yes, the poor will always be there, the scandal of the poor, and they will need to be ministered to, but there will also be the scandal of the waste of lives poured out in homage, in personal devotion to our Lord—for this is what Mary's gesture signifies: the total and unreasonable lavishing of the rich potential of a life.

As we sit quietly with the Lord and pour out upon him one of our most precious possessions, our time and the flow of our life, something within us cries: "Why this waste! This time could be spent in serving the terrible needs of the poor"—and what human is not poor! But what our Lord is proclaiming here is that he does want this kind of extravagance. He does want us to pour out ourselves on him personally, to no apparent profit, even to the apparent detriment of his beloved poor. This is a word we need to ponder.

I would like to point out another subtle word that is contained in this pericope. Some years ago, a prominent convert shared with me the story of her conversion. It began in the House of Representatives. The day had seen a very tense debate. It had been a long day, and a very tired and worn woman reached for her hat in the House cloakroom. As she did so, she overheard one representative saying to another: "Well, we can count on the Lord to take care of that." My friend turned to him and said: "I wish I could say that." The representative was on the ball. He replied: "Friend, if you go home and take down your Bible and read it as you would read a bill you are going to vote on in the House tomorrow, you will be able to say that." My friend went home, took down her Bible, blew off the dust, and began to read the Gospel as she would read a House bill. She read every word, and before every word and behind every word and above every word and below every word. Before she got very far through Matthew, she was seeking a priest to give her instructions.

The Fathers, in speaking about Scripture, often tell us we have to get beyond the rind of the obvious, literal sense to taste the sweet fruit of the spiritual sense; we have to break the shell of the nut to be nourished by the meat within. We need to question the text and read between the lines. A while ago, someone put a poem on my desk; it was entitled: *Fish*. The first line read: "What was Jesus doing while they were pulling in the nets?" You will immediately recognize the allusion to the day when Jesus had preached in Peter's boat and then told him and his companions to cast out the nets, and they took in a great haul. What was Jesus doing while Peter and his confreres were pulling in the nets?

In relation to our present text, I would ask: Where did Mary get that fabulously valuable jar of perfume? We might first have to ask, Who is this Mary? I would hold that this sister of Lazarus is the same as the sinful woman who had previously washed our Lord's feet with her tears, anointed them, and dried them with her hair, as she does here. We have something curious in this favored household. Contrary to the whole mores and indeed religious sense

of the times and the people, here is a wealthy family on the out-
skirts of the capital where we find three apparently unmarried persons. I think this might be explained by the fact that Mary, the sinful woman, had so disgraced the family that it was virtually impossible for her brother and sister to marry; especially when, in their
great charity, they received her back into their home. And I am sure
it would have been such compassionate love as this that so attracted
Jesus to this family. In any case, Mary has this extraordinary alabaster jar of perfume—from whence? Perhaps her brother bought
it for her as a sort of consolation gift. But that does not seem too
likely. It seems more likely that she had bought it for herself when
she was plying her trade, to lure customers; or perhaps it was the
payment she received from one of her clients. If so—the humility
of our God, to accept such a gift! And what does it say to us? No
matter how we have used and abused our power to love, no matter
how contaminated it might seem, yet he wants it, and the whole
of it.

The Lord does want our love, our prayer, that prayer of love in
which we pour ourselves out on him in extravagance. He values it,
and it will fill the whole Church. He values it, and we should value
it. And no matter how loudly the voices within us and outside us—
those eminently practical voices—cry out: Why this waste? we
should give it time and place. It should have a very high priority in
our lives.

One of the things that has impressed me about the teachers in
the TM movement has been the fidelity with which they have or-
dered priorities and have inculcated this in all they have taught.
Maharishi Mahesh Yogi wants to bring TM to the whole world and
to do this as quickly as possible. Yet always he has insisted on absolute fidelity to daily meditation by all and has periodically with-
drawn his teachers from the field to spend long periods in more intense meditation. I was struck the first time I telephoned and asked
for someone and the person on the phone replied that my party was
meditating at the moment—would I please call back in twenty minutes. I said to myself: Wow! Isn't that something! I have heard it
many times since. I certainly have not been offended by it. Far
from it. I have been edified. We see it as the obvious thing, once we

have set our priorities, and it is becoming the accepted thing in our society. A few times of late when I have been out, my host has politely asked if I wanted some time to meditate before supper, or has arranged the schedule so that I would have some free time then. At other times, when I have slipped away for twenty minutes of meditation when washing up before the meal, it has been taken as a matter of course. If we ourselves are arranging a meeting or a gathering, we should have the sensitivity and consideration to provide time and space for our guests or participants to meditate. It is really just common courtesy. And it often does offer the opportunity to speak with others about Centering Prayer and to share it with them.

If we are convinced that it is important for us to sit down quietly with the Lord a couple of times a day, we will make time for it. If I get an important long-distance call when I am on my way to supper or an engagement, I do not hesitate to take time for it even if I have to excuse myself and come a bit late. How important is prayer, how urgent is this meeting with the Lord?

Some have found it most helpful to put their Centering Prayer time right into the program of their daily schedule. The appointment book reads: 4:30—J.C. If we are fortunate enough to have a secretary, we can tell him or her we are not to be disturbed during that important appointment. If we are not so fortunate, we might have to put a note on our door and take the phone off the hook. [If the first number of the exchange is dialed, the phone will be silent and callers will get a busy signal, so they will know we are there and will call back later.]

We do not hesitate to give regular appointments to others. Is Jesus any less a person, with any less right to our time and attention? If I am busy with one of my brothers and another intrudes, I do not hesitate to ask him to return in fifteen minutes or whatever. It is understood and accepted. Occasionally the intruder has an urgent need. Then I excuse myself from the man I am engaged with and attend to him. I am equally free with the Lord. If there is an urgent need, I am sure he does not mind if I attend to it and come back to him later. But I should show him the same courtesy I show all my other brothers, and not readily set him aside during his appointed time.

One of the things that sometimes gets hold of us in ministry is the myth of availability. Total availability—always ready to respond to anyone at any time. We really are making too much of ourselves —and perhaps seeking a little ego satisfaction; we are so needed! Maybe it is *we* who *need* to be needed! The Lord can manage to take care of things sometimes without us. I have never yet met anyone who has been alienated because he or she has had to wait a bit because I was at prayer.

Actions speak louder than words. We can help others learn more surely the true hierarchy of values, the importance of prayer, the way to peace, by living it ourselves. Someone waiting at my door while I pray will probably learn more about prayer than if he or she were inside with me, talking about it. Of course it might even be better if he or she were inside with me, praying. We should not hesitate to invite others to sit with us in prayer. It is a very good way to begin an interview. If we believe "Where two or three are gathered in my name, there I am in the midst of them," it would be polite to give the Lord some attention. And it can lead to much peace.

My abbot shared this with me: When he is at home he has little difficulty finding time for his meditations. But he did find some difficulty when he was visiting other communities. So he decided at the beginning of a visit to announce that he would not be available for a half hour before lunch and supper. The reaction was universally favorable; the men were even impressed. He obviously believed what he taught. Actions do speak louder than words. And certainly one of the best things we can do for others is to teach them the priority of prayer and how they can get intimately in touch with God in the center of their own being and experience his great love for them.

When we really love someone, we look forward to being with him. An appointment with a loved one takes high priority. We do not readily let anything stand in its way. We go to it eagerly. At one of our workshops a monk shared this with us: He usually did his centering in a little house or hermitage he had in the garden.

He used to look forward during his afternoon's work to the time when he would be able to lay aside his tools and run to that rendezvous. And he would literally run there. He found that if, on a particular day, he was kind of high and dry and did not feel so eager, he would still run there, and by the time he arrived, the run would have restored his eagerness.

It is good to have a particular place where we usually meet with the Lord. The place itself will come to be more and more helpful to us in entering quickly into deep prayer. It will build up its own supportive "vibes." The presence of an icon or an open Bible can proclaim sacred space, a real Presence. A burning candle can proclaim sacred time. We need to get a better grasp on sacramentality and use it supportively. Yet this certainly remains true: we can center anyplace, anytime.

Another support to fidelity is accountability. To have a partner or a group with whom we can center regularly is a tremendous help. If we teach others, we realize the absolute necessity of being faithful ourselves so that we can teach authentically. And if we follow up our teaching, as is always most desirable, it gives us a support group that we in turn support. Married couples have obvious prayer partners, but they should be sensitive and carefully ascertain when it is truly mutually opportune. A married couple centering regularly together will discover their marital relation opening out on every level to new freedom and fullness. So many couples have shared the sacredness of this with me.

One of the great thrills I received this year was a Christmas letter from a married couple who had come to see me a couple weeks before the feast. I would like to share it with you:

Christmas Day, 1978

Dear Father Basil,

Thank you for your Christmas gift to us and our children. We held off writing this letter intentionally because we wanted to let you know how we fared within our family community first.

The first attempt at meditation was a week ago. Alice [the

writer's wife] had gone to work, and I asked Bernadette, Renee, Kieran and Colette [four of their children] if they would like to participate in a meditation. They had listened to our conversations about our visit to you and I guess they were curious. To my surprise they gave me an eager positive answer. Again I used Father Meninger's tape as the basis. At the end I sat quiet and let them fill in the conversation. Each talked in glowing terms about his own experience. How great it was. When Alice called, as was her wont, they told her how great it was.

On December 24th we did it again, but this time Vinnie [their eighteen-year-old son] and Alice were also present. How nice and peaceful the experience was. Alice and I were delighted with its reception. In fact we find it rather amazing that most of our friends have been complaining to us that their teenagers don't even want to go to church, let alone pray. This is somewhat frightening to us that God's Grace is doing this for us.

After all the gift-giving on Christmas Eve we sat down with our older children. The topic of conversation they brought up was prayer. Vinnie said that he was looking for a religious experience and it was not found in the local church. He also thought that this centering prayer was pretty "cool" and he felt pretty good while doing it. (To my surprise it was he that was in the living room this A. M. in the meditation position.) Bernadette said that she and a group of students at Marist are forming a prayer group and that the priest is letting them choose their own method or manner of prayer. Bernadette has just said she would like the tapes when she returns for the spring semester.

So you can see what you started, Father Basil. We are so glad you did and so glad that you shared your gift with us for this Christmas. I don't expect a response to this letter because you have a busy schedule. I'll try to keep you informed of the progress of the Confraternity class and if any problems arise. Alice and I are now planning a retreat with the House of

Prayer as mentioned in the pamphlet "Finding Grace at the Center." Thanks again.

Love,

Vin Murphy

Families that pray together, stay together!

It is good to be aware of the times and the seasons that can most easily undermine our practice. After a long period of fidelity, a relatively short period without centering can make it difficult for us to return to it. Perhaps it is a sense of guilt that we do not want to face. Periods that should leave us freest to center and would be most enhanced by extra centering, tend to be dangerous times for sloughing off. When we are on vacation and seeking to rest and be renewed, what could be more helpful than some extra hours of meditation? When we are sick in bed and seeking deeper rest and restoration, how helpful would be extra hours of deep quiet, in touch with the Source of all life and vitality! Yet it seems it is during these times many fall away from regular practice. Maybe it is due to the fact that we do not have to get our meditation in at a particular time, so we tend to get lax and not get it in at any time. What we miss when we miss a particular meditation, we will never know. It might have been the most beautiful experience of our lives. We cannot afford to miss a single such encounter with the Lord, for it is an eternal loss.

In saying what I just said, I do not want to give the false impression that if one cannot center twice a day he or she should not do it at all. Even if we did it only once a week it would be to the good. Every effort and realization of entering into deeper prayer and communion with God is precious. If we can manage only once a day, that is not as good as twice a day, certainly; yet it is a very precious thing and will have a transforming effect on our lives.

But I certainly would want to challenge a decision that we cannot make space in our lives for twenty minutes of meditation twice a day. In such a case I think we need to take a hard look at our values and our living out of them. If the way our lives are moving along is not in line with our deep hopes and aspirations, there will inevitably come a day of reckoning. If we spend days, weeks, months, years, getting pushed around by circumstances and people, or our own passions and emotions, instead of moving in some relaxed way toward the true goals of our lives, there will be a great backwash, a terrible sense of waste and failure.

Many times, the sudden shifts, the radical breaks we see in the lives of our brothers and sisters are due precisely to this. For years, their lives have been filled with the choppy shifting activities of surface motions, the buffeting of winds and the wake waves of others' motorboats instead of that deep, steady flow from the Source to the ocean of divine life, love, and joy. This may be happening largely unconsciously because they are living unexamined lives. This is the great value of having a rule of life, a spiritual guide or companion, periodical times of retreat and review. It may be, too, because of an unwillingness to pay the price of being deep persons. John Dunne, in the opening pages of his excellent study *Time and Myth* speaks to this:

> Nothing seems to remain. A man passes through the ages of life— childhood, youth, manhood, old age. Each age comes and goes, and life itself seems to go in death just as childhood does in youth and youth in manhood and manhood in age. Much the same thing seems to happen to whole civilizations. . . . Nothing seems to remain after life but a death mask, a cast taken from a dead face, an impression left by a once living being. An enduring life, a life that could last through and beyond death would have to be a deeper life than the ordinary. It would have to be some life that men have without knowing it, some current that runs far beneath the surface. To find it would be like seeing something fiery in the depths of life; it would be like hearing a rhythm in life that is not ordinarily heard. The question is whether a man, if he found such a life, could bear to live it, whether he could live at that depth, whether he could live according to that rhythm. The deeper life would be like an undertow, like a current that flows beneath the surface, a current that sets seaward or along the beach while the waves on the surface are breaking upon the shore. The phases of life and the phases of civilization are like the waves, each phase swelling and dying away, each

one rolling onto shore and breaking. A life lived on the surface is like the surf itself, like the swell of the sea that breaks upon the shore, like the foam, the splash, the sound of breaking waves. There is no swelling and breaking in the undertow, no foam, no splash, no sound. Yet it is a powerful current and may move in a direction opposite to that of the waves, may move toward the open sea while they move toward the shore. A man who gave himself to the deeper current of life might run a risk like that of a man who let himself be caught in the undertow. It might be better for him to float on the surface and let himself be carried in to shore. To live in accord with the deeper rhythm might be to ignore the surface rhythm of life. It might mean missing the normal joys and cares of childhood, youth, manhood, and age. It might mean plunging down into the depths of life to follow a light as elusive as sea fire.

It may well be more than a lack of time that holds us back from faithfully giving ourselves to Centering Prayer, though that is the common plaint I hear: "I would really like to, I really enjoy centering, but I just cannot give time to it in the afternoon. I just can't make the time."

One day our Lord was sitting in the temple opposite the treasury. He was watching the worshipers coming up and dropping their alms in the offering box. Suddenly he turned to his disciples who were sitting near him. "See that widow there!" Their gaze followed his gesture. "She has just dropped two mites into the coffer. But I tell you, she has given more than all the rest who have come. For they have given out of their superfluity, but she has given of her very substance, what she could not afford." The Lord most appreciates it when we give the time we really cannot afford to give. And he will show his appreciation. He will take care of things as only he can while we meditate. And he will so refresh us that we will soon find that we are getting a lot more done in less time and needing to give less time to sleep. Time given to contemplative prayer is time well invested, even on a natural level. Whenever anyone asks me how I manage to get so much done, I always answer: "By giving several hours a day to contemplative prayer."

In these pages I have emphasized Centering Prayer and making time for two regular periods a day. When we do this, we will soon enough find that it is creeping more and more into our lives. Many tell me how the periods grow longer, how they are beginning to take a little time each day after lunch—far better than a snooze—how the prayer word comes at quiet moments to invite them to enjoy a pause that refreshes. What we do want to move toward is a whole contemplative style and pace of life. We want to allow time for clouds and sunsets, for the beauty in faces and the little things of life.

The Greek Fathers distinguished between *chronos* and *chairos*. *Chronos* is chronological time: the steady flow of minutes, hours, days, and years. It moves along relentlessly, with steady, unflagging pace—no matter what is going on. It is totally equalitarian, flat, unvarying. *Chairos* is the time of grace, the fullness of the present moment, the all that is now. Each moment has its own uniqueness, its own fullness, its own quality. If we can enter into the school of Centering Prayer and are faithful to our lessons, we will, quicker than we expect, graduate into a life of *chairos*, a life that is filled with luminous Presence, great peace, a constancy in joy: a veritable beginning of life eternal here on earth. May the Divine Master lead us all swiftly through these lessons, forming in us the mind and heart of Christ.

X

SPREADING THE GOOD NEWS

We are all in mission. "Go forth and teach. . . ." This command of the Lord was meant not only for the Twelve but for us all, for we have all been baptized into Christ, the One who is sent. We are a royal priesthood, and as priests we are not only to stand before the Father, constantly making intercession, showing Christ's wounds, living the sacrifice of the Only-begotten, but, like him, we are to bear gifts to men from the Father, the gifts of life and truth. It is not only the unbaptized who need to be evangelized. We all need to hear, every day, ever more fully, the message, the Word of life. This is why the Liturgy of the Eucharist is always preceded by the Liturgy of the Word; this is why, each day, we need to encounter the living Word in our daily *lectio*.

We need to get more and more in touch with who we really are. "Christian, know your dignity," was the early Fathers' insistent charge. Again and again, in a baptizing context, they repeated the words of the Delphic oracle: *Know thyself*. For in knowing ourselves we come to know our God—in knowing ourselves who are made in his image and likeness. We are the most perfect reflection of God in creation. We are the expression and effect of God's love, and God is love.

A Protestant minister wrote recently:

> I look at the example of Jesus and I realize that's my possibility. . . . We are created in the image and likeness of God. And

running our patterns, playing our games and having our acts prevents us from living out the fullness of who we are.

I see that the task of the Church, and of my ministry, is to assist people in finding themselves in the image and likeness of God. We are asked to live out of the fullness of who we are. I'm sure that much of organized religion has failed a lot of people. Valid experiences have given rise to belief systems which are often passed on without experience and which then delineate what kind of experiences are "valid" in the future. Many of us have experienced a certain facet of the truth, and then we've gotten locked into it. We're not open to the total possibility. . . .

One of the best ways we can help others to come to know their true selves with their limitless potential to share divine life and happiness (after truly compassionate prayer) is to help them find the way to leave behind the entanglements of their false, superficial selves and come to their center, to the ground of their being, where they are constantly coming forth from the creative love of the Father. And this is precisely what the simple method of coming to presence, which we call Centering Prayer, is seeking to do. To share Centering Prayer with others is a preeminent way to fulfill our Christian mission, and to open out to our brothers and sisters the Way, the Truth, and the Life; that is, the Good News.

I can recall the first time that I came into a group to share Centering Prayer and discovered that it included a dark-skinned brother from India, one dressed in the white garb of a swami. I must confess I felt a twinge of discomfort, or was it fear? There has prevailed in our Western world such an inferiority complex in regard to spiritual practice that I am certainly not wholly free of it. I accept the insightful summation of Monsignor Rosanno, the secretary of the Vatican Secretariat for non-Christian Religions: "We share with our brothers and sisters of the East the mystical, spiritual and ascetical revelation (and we have to humbly confess that in many instances we have not lived it out as well as they have), but we have something more: the historical revelation. And it is our responsibility humbly to share this gift also with our brothers and sisters." Yet my feelings do not always wholly coincide with my convictions.

I presented the Centering Prayer in my usual way, wondering what chords of response this call to faith and love might be striking in the Hindu monk. We soon entered into the prayer and enjoyed that beautiful fullness of silence. As we came out of the experience I shot a concerned glance in the direction of our Eastern friend. He had—or, I could almost say, was—a most beautiful smile, a deep, radiant expression of peaceful joy. Gently he gave his witness: "This has been the most beautiful experience I have ever had." This was for me on many levels a very affirming experience. But affirmation is the constant effect of our sharing with others.

All of us have misgivings when we think of ourselves cast in the role of a teacher of prayer. We are only too conscious of our sins and miseries, our backsliding and infidelity; how much of our prayer seems to be just so much spaghetti: an endless tangle of thoughts, feelings, and imaginings. How dare we teach others?

But let us reflect for a moment on the call of the prophet Samuel. He was fortunate to be living at the time with a spiritual father—not the best, but one who had some knowledge of the ways of the Lord and discernment of them. One night, the Lord called the young man as he slept. (Many good things are recounted in the Bible as having happened during sleep; maybe the Lord wants to emphasize that it is really he who takes the initiative and we have but to do what he wants, when he wants it, even sleep.) Hearing his name, "Samuel, Samuel," the lad thought it was his spiritual father, Eli, calling, for he did not know as yet the ways of the Lord. So he jumped up and ran to his master: "Here I am, for you called me." Eli did not readily perceive what was going on (as I said, he wasn't the best of spiritual fathers), so he sent the lad back to bed. It was only at the third call that Eli finally realized it was the Lord and instructed Samuel how to respond.

Many today, like Samuel, are hearing the call of the Lord coming to them in various ways, some even a good bit more unconventional than a voice in the night. But they do not recognize the voice. They do not perceive what is going on. They do not know how to respond. This is where there is a great need for spiritual guides—even poor ones, like Eli and me and you. At least we can teach people *how to listen,* how to say, in the way they act more than in words, "Speak, Lord, for your servant wants to hear." Then the Lord can do the rest. He can pour his Spirit into their hearts—the Spirit whom he promised would teach them all things, even the deep things of God.

We will find if we dare to forget ourselves for the sake of our brothers and sisters, and to share ourselves, to lay down our lives, that the Lord himself will fill up what is wanting. He will make up for all our insufficiencies. He will make our words bearers of life. And while he gives to others through us, in response to their faith and ours, he will also give to us. We will not be just pipes, but reservoirs, giving out of the fullness we have received. Such is the mercy of God. We find the old adage to be very much our experience: the best way to learn is to teach.

One of my favorite success stories is that of a quiet little middle-aged sister who attended a Centering Prayer workshop one spring a few years ago. As usual, at the end of the workshop I exhorted the participants to go forth and share with others what they had received. "Freely have you received, freely give." Sister had hardly spoken up in the course of the workshop, and as she left she gently shook her head and thought, "Well, maybe someday I will be able to teach others, but that will be a long time coming."

I met sister about three weeks later, and she told me what had happened in the intervening days. She lived in an apartment with three other sisters. When she reached home that evening, the others were eager to hear what had happened. Before she knew it, the four of them were sitting there centering. The next day at the morning coffee break at the motherhouse, the question was the same: What happened at your workshop? And the result was the same; soon eleven were enjoying a prayer break instead of a coffee break as they sat together in silence. They agreed to meet in the lounge after work for a second experience. By the end of the week, ninety sisters were meeting in the lounge at four-thirty each day to center together. And they had made a pact that they would not come to work in the morning without first having centered for half an hour.

When I met sister about three weeks after her workshop, the sisters were making plans as to how they might get to the other six thousand in their congregation in the course of the summer.

During that same summer, a young Jewish convert, a professor at a Catholic college, visited the monastery. He was deeply touched by Centering Prayer, and in September he organized a weekend workshop for six faculty members and seven students. The day after the workshop ended, the students went through all the dormitories on campus and invited every student personally to an introductory lecture on "Christian Meditation." The response was very strong, and during the following weekends a great number were introduced to the practice. A half dozen meditation rooms were set up around the campus, with set times for group meditations in each and the freedom to use the rooms at any time for private meditation. After the initial sharing of the lay professor, the students took all the initiative.

I think one of the great failures in very many of our Christian communities has been that we have asked too little, expected too little, from young adults. We could all learn something from the Church of Jesus Christ of Latter-day Saints in this regard. Also from Maharishi Mahesh Yogi, who built up a vast meditation movement in a very few years, beginning with virtually no resources but relying heavily on the good zeal and sense of mission of collegians. A very considerable percentage of the leadership of the Transcendental Meditation (TM) movement has been young men and women who have grown up in the Christian churches. Whenever we teach or share Centering Prayer with others, we should not fail to encourage them to go forth and do likewise. The responsibility of teaching others encourages us to ever greater fidelity, as does, certainly, setting up support groups and working out follow-up programs.

In teaching Centering Prayer, the simpler the presentation the better. It is usually better to answer questions only *after* the experience. In this way, the teaching can be more relevant to the actual need for information of the persons learning. And we will not burden people with a lot of information that they personally do not need or want. Nor will we waste our time answering the pseudo problems that arise from *a priori* thinking about something that is essentially nonconceptual and experiential.

The best workshop is one that allows ample time for actual meditation, both in groups and individually, and for sharing and questions that flow out of experience. It is well for the workshop also to include some practical consideration of *lectio* as a support of one's practice; of how to formulate a personal rule of life; of ways of sharing and teaching others, and of follow-up. In an appendix to this chapter I will include some sample programs for workshops and follow-up sessions.

Follow-up is very important. When we first began teaching Centering Prayer in our retreat house, there was a natural structure for follow-up, as those learning could easily return for another retreat, with the opportunity to pray again with a group and to discuss this kind of prayer. But when we began to conduct workshops outside, such an opportunity was not immediately present. However, at the very first workshop, there arose a spontaneous demand for some sort of follow-up program. That particular group, since they all came from a relatively confined geographic area, decided to meet bimonthly for a twenty-four-hour get-together. In the ensuing months and years, they found this regular reunion one of the most supportive elements in their busy lives.

Over the years, I have seen groups come up with a great variety of plans in order to provide follow-up support for themselves, sometimes at great personal cost and sacrifice on the part of the members of the group. Without some support of this kind at least initially, most seemed to realize, there would be little hope of their efficaciously integrating this practice into their daily lives, no matter how good and fruitful they actually found it to be.

Other schools of meditation have realized such a need and have worked out communal arrangements and tightly structured programs. One might draw ideas from some of these in elaborating his or her own program. For example, in the Transcendental Meditation movement, the actual teaching of the practice is preceded by a couple of introductory lectures, so that only those who really want to enter into the way of meditation are taught. A fee is charged—some think it is exorbitant, but it does impress on the recipient that what he is receiving is of value and that he should prize it and not set it aside lightly. I am not suggesting that in teaching Centering Prayer one should begin charging fees, although weekend programs do have their reasonable expenses to be covered. But it might not be a bad idea to require something of the recipients, perhaps a couple of days of free service to a local charity, some hospital or prison visits, or some other spiritual or corporal work of mercy.

In the TM program, after one has been initiated or taught, he or she is required to return each day for three days, for group meditation and additional input. Then, through the ensuing month, one is expected to come once a week, and through the year, at least once a month. This is considered minimal. Many advance lectures and intensive weekends are offered. It was not in imitation of this but in response to a very real and strongly expressed need that we developed the advanced workshop. The TM program was undoubtedly elaborated in response to the same need.

I think it will always be true that some find meditating in a group more supportive than others. I suspect this depends in good part on the individual's psychological makeup. Some are more private persons and always find the presence of others distracting and to some degree discomforting. Others find togetherness most supportive. It is undoubtedly true, though, that when a group meditates together, even when there are only two, the responsibility to each other promotes fidelity. Moreover, there is set up a climate of prayer, a flow of hidden grace, which at times is almost palpable, that strengthens the meditation of each and creates a deep bonding in Christian community.

A Centering Prayer program can grow on its own, or it can go in tandem with an already existing one. An example of the former is that found in a few parishes. As Lent opened, the pastors announced in their parish bulletins that during Lent they would offer the opportunity to members of the parish to learn a simple method of deeper prayer or contemplative prayer that belongs to our Christian tradition. In all cases, the pastors were surprised by the large turnouts they had to handle. It provided a real opportunity to call forth some of the laity to share in leadership. Once a week during the holy season, the pastor gave conferences largely of the type found in the introductory workshop and led the group in the experience of Centering Prayer. By the time Lent was over, the regular weekly meeting for Centering Prayer was under way. At each meeting, during the first half hour (actually sort of a premeeting half hour from seven-thirty to eight), instruction was given to newcomers. Then the whole group meditated for twenty minutes or half an hour. After this there was time for questions and sharing of experiences. Usually there was also some Scripture sharing before the social. Being able to come together weekly, sharing, having doubts or questions answered, being with others in this experience of God, greatly facilitated fidelity to practice. And in the parishes where this has been established, it has provided a much desired alternative for those who are not attracted to the more extroverted prayer experience usually found in parish charismatic prayer groups. As in the charismatic movement, individuals have been able to establish small group meetings in their homes and neighborhoods, and members have been able to carry Centering Prayer into other sectors of their lives, to offices, campuses, hospitals, and service centers.

For some who have looked on the charismatic movement with a certain longing, wanting a renewed and experiential prayer life supported by a group, yet not feeling comfortable with such outspoken and demonstrative devotion, Centering Prayer groups have been literally an answer to prayer. For others, however, Centering Prayer has not been an alternative to charismatic prayer but something flowering forth from it, the two being very much part of an integral prayer life. Obviously when Christians are at the moment when the Spirit is calling them forth to a very strong affective prayer that joyously expresses itself in song, dance, tongues, and prophecy, it is not the time to try to get such sons and daughters of the Father to sit down and quietly center. There is a time and a season. It is not uncommon that after one has been in the charismatic experience for some time, he or she begins to experience a call to more and more quiet. *Be still and know that I am God.* It is at this point that it is most helpful if the leadership of the prayer group is able to give some guidance, and perhaps help the member to enter more fully into this call of grace by sharing with him or her the Centering Prayer method.

In one diocese, Centering Prayer workshops have been conducted for the leaders of all the prayer groups. At the large Eastern General Meeting of Charismatics in Atlantic City in October 1978, Father William Meninger offered to teach Centering Prayer, restricting his audience to those who had been in the charismatic movement for at least two years and were actually leaders of prayer groups. Over a thousand crowded into a hall meant for only seven hundred. How many more were unable to get in, I don't know. It was an awesome experience to feel a thousand lovers sitting together in silence with their Beloved.

In some local charismatic meetings they now have the practice, after the general meeting each week, of offering a Centering Prayer session, in which the members whose lives are beginning to open out to the contemplative dimension can receive instruction, and all who wish can share, have questions answered, and have some time to pray together in holy silence.

One often asks the question or expresses the concern: Is this type of prayer open to everyone? I would not deny the validity of the criteria of St. John of the Cross for discerning when one is called to contemplative prayer. But, as I have previously stated, I think his criteria are fulfilled far more readily than we were wont to suspect.

Ordinarily, if we are going to have the opportunity to share with a brother or sister over a prolonged period of time, we will first want to foster the growth of faith on the conceptual and affective level through a living encounter with Christ in his inspired Word. As our Lord reveals his love and lovableness, there quite naturally, as it were, grows a desire for more intimate experience of him. This, then, is the time to open to contemplative experience through Centering Prayer.

But at times we find ourselves in a quite different situation. I think of the occasion when a chance conversation opens to a request: Could you teach me Christian meditation? Or perhaps a man or woman of only remote Christian background or none at all, who has been a pilgrim and a seeker, comes to our door with the same request. This may be a unique opportunity. There may be little hope of seeing this person again, unless grace in some very special way touches him or her in the course of the encounter or subsequently through what it brings into his or her life. What are we to do? I will tell you what I do.

I have the person sit down, and then in the simplest way possible teach the method of Centering Prayer. Then we center together. (I think it is of fundamental importance that whenever we teach Centering Prayer we immediately do it with those whom we are teaching. It is often best not even to allow any questions until after the experience, for this prayer is a thing of experience and can only be known and understood, insofar as it can be understood, through personal experience.) And we should be very sure that when doing the prayer with someone we do pray and not spend the time wondering how he or she is making out, because the best way to support another's prayer is to enter into deep prayer ourselves. In this way, we create a supportive environment.

However, since this person does not have a living faith at the moment, rather than tell him to choose a meaningful word, I suggest that he use the holy Name of Jesus. Usually I find that a person in this situation has a good experience, for he is truly open and seeking. Two particular results flow from this: The person has some confidence in me as a teacher and knows Jesus has something to do with what is going on. I then present my friend with a small New Testament or a copy of the Gospel of St. John. I try to impress upon him that this is a very sacred book and he must treat it with greatest reverence; and I ask him to spend at least ten minutes every day listening to it. Usually I will learn that the person has read the whole book in the first sitting. But he will take up the practice he has been taught: two twenty-minute sessions of Centering Prayer (here, too, there is a tendency to overdo, and the neophyte should be warned not to go too far in this) and ten minutes of listening to the Word of God. Faith comes through hearing. The centering is true prayer, for even if God be for the moment an unknown God, our friend is truly seeking him. And the daily Scriptures will soon enough reveal to him who it is he is finding in his prayer.

Since encounters such as these happen by chance, in most cases I do not have the joy of knowing all that the Lord has worked through them, but the indications I have received have been a cause of joy and thanksgiving.

I personally think Centering Prayer can be taught to everyone. The purity and simplicity of the method can lend itself to various expressions, and in practice actually does. When teaching Centering Prayer, I like to quote those words of Dom Chapman that my spiritual father used to quote to me: "Pray as you can, don't pray as you can't." We should go to prayer without any expectations. We seek the Lord. If we do not have that desire within us, we find ourselves spending more time working on that, and our prayer will tend to be more conceptual and affective. But if we keep it in the framework of the Centering Prayer, it will always tend toward greater depth and purity, while we will begin to draw more from the Liturgy of the Word, from our own *lectio*, and from the aspirations of the day to supply our conceptual and affective needs in prayer. It is very important always to keep in mind the words of the author of *The Cloud of Unknowing*: ". . . never strain your mind or imagination, for truly you will not succeed in this way."

While I think it is true that Centering Prayer *can* be taught to all, I do not want to suggest that it actually *be* taught to everyone, though I would certainly like to see it made available to all. I definitely do not like to teach Centering Prayer to a "captive audience." In a situation where I have been invited to make a presentation on Centering Prayer to a class, an organization, a retreat group, or the like, I much prefer to give a general introductory talk, showing the place of contemplative prayer in the life of the individual and in the tradition of the Western Christian community, and then invite those who would be interested to take part in a session in which they may actually learn and experience Centering Prayer. Even then, and in workshops specifically brought together to learn Centering Prayer, I like to stress that one should not try to force oneself into a specific mold of prayer. Each should pray as he can, following the movement of the grace of the Holy Spirit. "We do not know how to pray as we ought, but the Spirit prays in us." I do, though, encourage participants, especially those in ministry, to give the method a fair chance to reveal its value to them. I encourage them to pray faithfully this way twice a day for a month. Then, at the end of the month, let them examine the matter with their spiritual father or mother. If they find in fact that the way they were previously praying was more satisfying and fruitful for them, then they should certainly return to it. They will surely lose nothing by the month's practice, for in truth they were truly seeking God in all. They now know Centering Prayer from personal experience, and it is readily available to them if at some future date it seems the suitable prayer for them. They will be able to better understand others who talk about this kind of prayer, and if such be their role, they will be better able to give guidance in the matter.

In general, I think it is very good for those of us who are in ministry to have personal experience of the various forms of prayer, and an ability to join in with those we serve in their respective forms; to be able to go to a charismatic meeting and enter into charismatic prayer; to a Quaker meeting and enter into Quaker prayer. I think it is good for us to know something, from the inside, about TM and Zen and Yoga and so on. At the same time, though, each must find the forms of prayer that truly serve to nourish and foster his own spiritual growth and be very faithful in the practice of them.

At times in sharing the Centering Prayer, we will find that some will have already discovered it for themselves. Their conversation with the Lord had just quieted down to a point where they were content simply to be in presence. They may center on the indwelling presence, or perhaps the object of their centering has been the tabernacle or the monstrance or a particular picture or icon or just the beads slipping through their fingers. Excellent! They are to be wholly affirmed and encouraged in their fruitful practice. In practice, the best way for each one to pray is always the way in which the Spirit leads, the way that works, the way that really keeps him in touch with God and with himself.

The absolutely important thing is that we do pray and pray regularly with as much sincerity and integrity as we can muster. Then we can be sure that we will be true to ourselves and that the Lord will accomplish in and through our prayer all he wishes to accomplish in our own lives and in the life of the whole Church.

How about the very young? Can we open out a contemplative dimension of life to them through Centering Prayer? When I first began sharing Centering Prayer with a larger audience, I received many surprises in this regard. First it was the brothers who told me how they were teaching Centering Prayer in high school. This was not too much of a surprise, for I knew that TM and other Eastern methods had been taught to younger people. Then the sisters began to report on their experience in grade school. Sister Ursula, with her sixth-graders, starts off each day with twenty minutes of Centering Prayer. If for some reason the class is prevented from doing this, they pester sister all day till they have had their meditation. They do it on their own on the weekends and report back on their experience.

I should think that this kind of prayer could not only be attractive to young people but greatly help them in working through their identity struggles. Adolescents often like to go off by themselves to "get in touch" and just kind of "be with" things. To give them a little method to do this and to give them a sense of God's presence, that in some way Jesus is with them and they have in him a loving and caring friend, can be a priceless gift.

Lower grades have tended to use shorter periods. The sisters feel that children are naturally contemplative, and if one could build on this natural ability there would not be such a struggle later on to reestablish a contemplative dimension in life. A minister friend bore witness to this when he wrote:

> I learned to center when I was six or seven years old—to just say, "Okay, Lord, what do you want to tell me?" And be still, and see what came. Although I didn't know it at the time, it was like getting into a process. I have found that the only way I can really function is from that rootedness or centeredness—that I act freely when I am turned in and centered in God, who is "the Beyond within."

The most fascinating report I have received is that from a mother. Each day, she gets her growing family off to school and work. Then she and her three-year-old sit side by side in their meditation chairs for twenty minutes, after which they play together for at least twenty minutes. At the point when the mother was reporting to me, it was the little one who was usually the first to get to the meditation chairs. The mother's gentle explorations indicated to her that her child was indeed enjoying some very beautiful experiences of his heavenly Father's enfolding love.

A few years ago, I was flying into New Orleans to do a report and presentation on Centering Prayer for the Conference of Major Superiors of Men Religious. I arrived at suppertime, and the parish near the airport was kind enough to offer me hospitality for the night. As we supped, I shared with my hosts the purpose of my visit. The parish team (about nine or ten in all, priests, religious, and lay) immediately became interested. They asked if I could not do a workshop for them. I explained that I had to be at the Major Superiors' meeting at nine in the morning. That was all right; we could begin right after supper and resume at five-thirty in the morning, they said.

This mini-workshop proved to be a most memorable one both for the beauty of the experience and for its fruitfulness. As we emerged from the first experience, one of the sisters had an especially tender glow about her. Her name was Sister Petronila, but all called her Pet. I had just met Pet along with the others and knew nothing of her situation, but I asked: "You must have had a very beautiful experience, Pet?" "Yes," she replied, "this is the first time in months I have been able to forget my pain." Sister was dying of an especially painful bone cancer. When I next saw her, about five months later and two months before her death, on Our Lady's Birthday, sister told me how this grace of contemplative prayer had turned the intervening months into a beginning of what was to come. I am sure it was in large part due to Sister Petronila that this parish team pursued centering with a special attentiveness until in time virtually the whole parish was centering, and it became a part of their regular celebration of the Liturgy.

In the reading at today's liturgy our Lord asked: "To what shall I compare the reign of God?" And he gave the answer: "It is like yeast which a woman took and kneaded into three measures of flour until the whole mass of dough began to rise." The grace we have received, which has opened out for us the contemplative dimension of our lives, is the wholesome yeast of the Lord. It is meant not only to leaven our own lives but also to be shared until it leavens the whole, until the whole mass, the whole Body of Christ, rises to a fuller enjoyment of the Divine Life, to which it is called. And that's why I like to insist very strongly that after having entered into this prayer personally, one should begin to share it with others. In a certain sense, this is an obligation. We are to love our neighbor as ourselves. If we have in fact found this prayer to be such a good thing in our own lives, then we have an obligation to seek to share it with our neighbors.

It is indeed good news that, at any moment we need or desire, we can very simply enter into ourselves and find there a place of deep peace and joy, a place where dwells the Source of all good, all life, all strength; an ever-faithful Love that totally affirms us with the gift of being and life, and the promise of eternal life. Let us open this reality to as many as we can. Let us lay down our lives for others by freely sharing their deepest meaning, their richest content—the constant abiding oneness that is ours with the very God of Love.

When we learn Centering Prayer, it is as though a new seed has been planted in our life's field. Do you remember this scene: Our Lord was sitting in Simon Peter's boat, a little distance from the shore. As he looked out over the crowd that had assembled to hear his words, his eyes climbed the hill beyond. It had been sown some months earlier. Now a clear trodden path stood out among the waving stalks of wheat. Along the edge of the field, among the rocks, dry headless stalks also waved in the wind, but those caught among the brambles, equally headless, were not able to stir—fruitfulness had been choked out of them. But, across the open field, the stalks heavily burdened with their fruit bowed gracefully in the breeze. And our Lord, ever so alive to the beauty and richness of his Father's work, seized upon the scene to teach a lesson.

The question now is: What is going to become of the seed of prayer that has been sown in our lives? Is it going to be something that will be quickly plucked out of our lives, leaving no trace as we scurry back and forth in our daily search for meaning? Or will our initial enthusiasm allow it to spring up, while our want of discipline permits it to be poorly rooted through want of *lectio* and faith sharing? Or will the pressure of so many things to do and the lack of a rule of life mean that it will be choked off—as the Wise Man says, "the fascination of trifles obscures the good"? Or will it spring up, well rooted, with its own space, and bear fruit thirty, sixty or a hundredfold? I believe when we hear this parable we tend to think that our Lord is speaking only of the fruitfulness of the seed in our own lives. But that is not really the case. Our Lord is here speaking of how we bring forth the life-giving seed in the lives of others. Unless the grain of wheat falls into the ground and dies, *it remains itself alone.* But if it dies, it yields. That thirtyfold is thirty others, or sixty others, or a hundred others. The grain itself becomes a beautiful plant, able to give life. It has come to fullness. It has come to maturity. It can be a spiritual father or a spiritual mother generating spiritual life in others. Every grain on the stalk of that wheat plant is "another," who in his or her turn can die to self and come alive and bring life to others. The grain of wheat falls into the ground and dies and grows up into a new wheat plant. It is a fine, hearty plant. But we expect something more than that. We expect it to have lots of other new grains.

Something happened to our corn this year. Many of the beautiful big cornstalks didn't have a single ear of corn on them. So what was the use of all their growing, occupying the ground, eating up all those nutrients? We could enjoy the sight of the deceptive scene, but little more. We were deceived. If they had borne but one single kernel, a single truncated ear, that kernel in its turn could have fallen into the ground, died and come up, and borne a dozen or more good ears, and on each there would have been hundreds of new kernels. In the same way, we are to get all sorts of groups going and then encourage each to die to self and rise again, and so on. The parable of the seed—we have received the seed and we are growing. . . .

I would like to end this chapter by sharing with you a letter I received in yesterday's mail:

> Peace and joy in our Lord Jesus Christ! One of the graces of my Centering Retreat was an increase in the time I spend contemplating. I went from twenty minutes to sixty minutes a day and

with His grace I have been faithful: thirty minutes in the morning and thirty in the afternoon. Yes, I've been teaching it, and still can't keep up with the demand. Praise God!

Everything is given to me in contemplation because He is everything and there is no proclamation without contemplation. The desire to be with Him keeps increasing. It is like a fire. Teaching Centering allows me to proclaim that "my Beloved is mine and I am His." Recently I taught sixty religious. Now, as I said, my alcoholics are taught [this woman's ministry is to an alcoholic program] if they wish, as well as any staff member. What a gift to be able to share!

APPENDIX

We have here a sampling of programs used at workshops of various lengths. In brackets I have indicated the chapters in this book that might provide the material for the various conferences or presentations.

By way of explanation:

Spiritual accompaniment refers to the practice of placing the participants in partnership. One of the ways we have done this is as follows: After the introductory conference inviting the participants to open to the Lord, they have been invited to write their names on cards and place them in a paten before the enthroned Bible. A conference is then given on the importance and value of having someone walk with us on our spiritual journey. At this point, reminding the members that when we give ourselves to the Lord we necessarily give ourselves to each other, I draw out the names from the paten two at a time and send the persons off as partners for the workshop and, I urge, beyond. The partners are asked to pray especially for each other, to pray together for the whole group, and to share their faith and experience as the workshop unfolds.

Centering Liturgy is a Eucharistic Liturgy that includes a period of Centering Prayer, usually during the Preparatory Rite, although it may be placed at some other time in the Liturgy.

FOUR-DAY WORKSHOP

Monday   4:00   Arrival
                5:00   Reception
                6:00   Supper
                7:30   Opening conference [It's Beyond Us—Yet
                             Ours]
                         Spiritual accompaniment
                         Evening prayer

Tuesday   Rise early enough for private prayer and reading
                7:30   Morning prayer
                8:00   Breakfast
                         Private prayer and reading, sharing with
                             partner
                10:30   Introduction to Centering Prayer [A New
                             Packaging]
                12:30   Lunch
                         Rest, private prayer and reading, sharing
                             with partner
                4:30   Centering Liturgy
                6:00   Supper
                7:30   Questions, sharing, discussion on Center-
                             ing Prayer

Wednesday   Rise early enough for centering and reading
                7:30   Morning prayer
                8:00   Breakfast
                         Private prayer and reading, sharing with
                             partner
                10:30   Group centering
                         Conference: Faith building [Fire in the
                             Heart]

	12:30	Lunch
		Rest, private prayer and reading, sharing with partner
	4:30	Centering Liturgy
	6:00	Supper
	7:30	Conference: Fruits of Centering Prayer [A School of Compassion]

Thursday		Rise early enough for centering and reading
	7:30	Morning prayer
	8:00	Breakfast
		Private prayer and reading, sharing with partner
	10:30	Group centering
		Conference: faith planning [Keeping the Light of Tabor]
	12:30	Lunch
		Rest, private prayer and reading, sharing with partner
	4:30	Centering Liturgy
	6:00	Supper
	7:30	Conference: Mary, model of faith [Mary, at the Heart of Things]

Friday		Rise early enough for centering and reading
	7:30	Morning prayer
	8:00	Breakfast
		Private prayer and reading, sharing with partner
	10:00	Evaluation
		Centering Liturgy
	12:30	Lunch

THREE-DAY WORKSHOP

Thursday	6:00	Supper
	8:00	Opening conference [It's Beyond Us—Yet Ours]
		Spiritual accompaniment
Friday	6:30	Morning Office
		Breakfast
		Private prayer and reading, sharing with partner
	10:00	Introduction to Centering Prayer [A New Packaging]
	12:00	Midday Office
		Lunch
		Rest, private prayer and reading, sharing with partner
	3:30	Group centering—sharing
	5:00	Eucharist
		Supper
		Vespers
	8:00	Discussion on Centering Prayer
Saturday		Rise early enough to center
	6:30	Morning Office
		Breakfast
		Private prayer and reading, sharing with partner
	10:00	Faith-building—dialogical reading [Fire in the Heart]
	12:00	Midday Office
		Lunch

                       Rest, private prayer and reading, sharing
                           with partner
          3:30   Group centering—sharing
          5:00   Eucharist
                       Supper
                       Vespers
          8:00   Faith planning [Keeping the Light of
                           Tabor]
                       Reflections on Mary [Mary, at the Heart of
                           Things]

Sunday   Rise early enough to center
          6:30   Morning Office
                       Breakfast
                       Private prayer and reading, sharing with
                           partner
          9:30   Evaluation
                       Centering Liturgy
          12:00   Midday prayer
                       Lunch

(This workshop works well for a long weekend: Thursday to Sunday or Friday to Monday.)

FORTY-EIGHT-HOUR WORKSHOP

Friday	4:30	Reception
	6:00	Supper
	7:15	Opening conference [It's Beyond Us—Yet Ours]
		Spiritual accompaniment
		Evening prayer

Saturday	Breakfast—Please help yourself at any time.
	8:30	Morning prayer
	10:15	Introduction to Centering Prayer [A New Packaging]
	12:15	Lunch
	3:30	Questions, sharing, discussion
	5:00	Centering Liturgy
	6:00	Supper
	7:15	Faith-building [To Be Who We Are; Fire in the Heart]
		Evening prayer

Sunday	Breakfast—as yesterday
	8:30	Morning prayer
	10:15	Twice a day [Keeping the Light of Tabor]
		Go, Teach All . . . [Spreading the Good News]
	12:15	Lunch
	2:00	Centering Liturgy

Let us try to foster a climate of prayer and quiet, so that these days can be days of rest and refreshment for all.

TWENTY-FOUR-HOUR WORKSHOP

Saturday   2:00   Opening—scripture sharing [It's Beyond
                        Us—Yet Ours]
                       Introduction to Centering Prayer [A New
                        Packaging]
               4:00   Tea
               4:30   Questions, sharing, discussion
               6:00   Supper
               8:00   Faith-sharing—accountability partnership
                       Evening prayer

Sunday   Rise early enough for Centering Prayer and reading
               7:30   Morning prayer
               8:00   Breakfast
                       Private prayer; sharing with partner
              10:00   Sacred reading [Fire in the Heart]
              11:00   Centering Liturgy
              12:30   Lunch
               1:15   Faith-planning [Keeping the Light of
                        Tabor]
                       Closing

ONE-DAY WORKSHOP

9:00   Introduction: a baptismal reality: "You are
       my son . . . [To Be Who We Are]
       Forming the Mind of Christ-Son [Fire in
       the Heart]
10:00 Tea and coffee
10:15 Christ experience: introduction to Cen-
       tering Prayer [A New Packaging]
11:30 Small-group discussion and sharing
12:30 Lunch
2:00   General sharing, questions, responses
       Return to the center: group meditation
4:30   Eucharist

EVENING WORKSHOP

4:30   Scripture sharing [It's Beyond Us—Yet Ours]

5:00   Introduction to Centering Prayer [A New Packaging]

6:15   Supper

7:30   Questions, sharing, discussion

8:30   Keeping the Light of Tabor

FORTY-EIGHT-HOUR FOLLOW-UP

Friday   4:00   Centering Liturgy
                  6:00   Supper
                  7:15   Sharing (of each one's experience in the
                          prayer and in teaching others)

Saturday   Breakfast—Please help yourself at any time.
                  8:30   Morning prayer
                  10:15   Group centering
                          Thoughts, thoughts, and more thoughts
                  12:15   Lunch
                  2:30   Rounding (four successive meditations,
                          with a short meditative walk between
                          the meditations)
                  5:00   Eucharistic Liturgy
                  6:00   Supper
                  7:15   Sharing

Sunday   Breakfast—as yesterday
                  8:30   Morning prayer
                          Group centering
                  10:15   Discussion: twice a day [Keeping the
                          Light of Tabor] Go, teach all . . .
                          [Spreading the Good News]
                  12:15   Lunch
                  2:00   Centering Liturgy

ADVANCED CENTERING PRAYER WORKSHOP-RETREAT

Monday	5:00	Arrival, reception
	6:00	Supper
	8:00	Opening Session*
Tuesday	6:45	Morning prayer, Liturgy
Wednesday	8:00	Breakfast
Thursday	10:15	Group centering
		Conference [To Be Who We Are; Thoughts, Thoughts, and More Thoughts; Progress in Centering Prayer; A School of Compassion; Keeping the Light of Tabor; Spreading the Good News]
	12:15	Lunch

* At the opening session, after the participants have introduced themselves and shared how they got started in Centering Prayer and what they hope to get out of the Advanced Workshop-Retreat, the aims of the Advanced Workshop are explained:

1. To intensify the experience of Centering Prayer for the participants.
2. To share the experience of Centering Prayer with those who have been practicing it for an extended period of time.
3. To broaden the conceptual and intellectual background for the Centering Prayer.
   Taped conferences on the history of contemplative prayer in the Christian tradition are played during meals. There are also a presentation and discussion on methods of meditating from Eastern traditions and how these might be integrated into Christian prayer.
4. To find means to support, sustain, and renew the practice of Centering Prayer after returning back home.
5. To develop confidence in teaching the Centering Prayer to others by deepening one's own practice and theological understanding of it.

2:30   Rounding (four successive meditations with a short meditative walk in between the successive meditations)

5:40   Evening prayer

6:00   Supper

7:30   Sharing of experiences
       Scripture sharing
       Compline

Friday   The workshop-retreat ends with breakfast.

XI

FIRE IN THE HEART

It might well have been one of those exhilarating mornings of early April when the warm sun, the freshness of nature, the sounds of wing and paw, definitely proclaim that the cold and wet of winter are finally gone. But the two young men who made their way along the descending road from Jerusalem toward the coastal plain reflected none of this exhilaration. Indeed, their spirits, reflected in their faces, gestures, and gait, were also definitely on the descent. They "had hoped." Like so many of our own day—young and not so young—they had made the journey to the feet of a Master. They "had hoped" at last to discover the full meaning of life. They "had hoped" to find the way to peace, to inner tranquillity, to transcendent fullness. They had heard a lot about the Master, wonderful things: his signs, his wonders, his compassion, his strength, his love, his words of life. But now it was all over.

They had had hopes, but they also had had expectations, with preconceptions—their own ideas of what the Master should be like, what he should say and do, how he should act. But it didn't come off. Yes, there were the wonderful moments, like last Sunday, when everybody finally seemed to see that he was *the one*—except, of course, those blind, conceited Pharisees. How wonderful it was! Even the stones seemed to cry out. And with what inspiring and almost terrifying energy he had cleared those profiteers out of the holy place! How many had been healed! How he had put the Sad-

ducees and Pharisees and Herodians in their place! What teaching!
It was great!

But then . . . all of a sudden it was over. It didn't add up. Perhaps in some way all were duped. And now these stories of a missing body, angels, visions. . . . No! They "had hoped," but they
weren't going to be duped again. And so they walked downhill
with downhill spirits.

And then something happened. One "opened the Scriptures to
them." And then they recognized him in the breaking of the bread.
Then they knew that the stranger who walked with them, who
talked with them, was the Lord, the Master, the one in whom they
"had hoped." And they hoped again. And soon they were on the
uphill road, with uphill spirits, hastening to join the Church in the
joyful proclamation: "He is risen indeed! and has appeared to
Peter."

The two young men could recognize the Master in the breaking
of the bread, in the Companion on the road, only because one
had "opened the Scriptures to them." We can't help thinking:
"Wouldn't it be wonderful to have Jesus open the Scriptures for
us!" But note what the two say: "Weren't our hearts burning within
us as he spoke to us on the way and opened the Scriptures to us?"

It was the Spirit of Jesus, the Holy Spirit, dwelling in their
hearts, who made Jesus' words fire for them—fire and light. Many
had heard Jesus' words. These two had heard them many times.
And in the end they walked away dispirited. But, at the Supper,
Jesus had promised he would send his Spirit and the Spirit would
teach us all, from within, with transforming fire. We, right now,
have that same Spirit, Jesus' Holy Spirit, in our hearts. And if we
will but open our Bibles and listen, he will teach us from within,
and our hearts, too, will burn within us.

I would like to share with you here, very briefly, a method of *lectio divina*—divine reading, godly reading, or perhaps we could say,
reading with God, with the Holy Spirit—walking with Jesus on the
way and letting his Spirit within us set our hearts ablaze as the
Scriptures are opened to us. This little method, which we find
spoken of in our tradition from as early as the fourth century, and it
probably goes back to the earliest days, is more than reading; it is

prayer, a real communication with God that opens out to us the depths and the heights—the depths of intimacy, the heights of transcendent contemplation.

First, we take our Bibles. We should always treat our Bibles with great reverence. They should not be simply put on the shelf with all the other books, or tossed on the desk. They should be enthroned in our homes, in our rooms. You see in many churches today the Sacred Text given a special place, sometimes with a lamp burning before it, proclaiming a real Presence—for God is truly present in his Word, waiting to speak to us and inflame our hearts.

So we begin this method of sacred reading, of encounter with the Lord, by taking our Bible and reverencing it. We might kiss the book, or kneel before it for a moment, or just hold it reverently in our hands—making a fully human act of reverence, bringing the body into it. Then, having become fully aware of the Presence, we take a moment to ask the Holy Spirit dwelling in us to help us really hear the Lord as he speaks to us now—to set fire to our hearts.

Now, ready, we begin to listen, setting for ourselves, say, ten minutes of time. It is not a question of reading a paragraph, a page, or a chapter. It is, rather, sitting down with a Friend, the Lord, and letting him speak to us. We listen. And if what he says in the first word or the first sentence strikes us, we stop and let it sink in. We relish it. We respond from our heart. We enjoy it to the full before we move on. There is no hurry. We are sitting with our Friend for ten minutes—and who cannot afford to give his or her best Friend ten minutes in the course of the day? We let him speak. We really listen. How often has our prayer been monological! We have done all the talking, expecting him to listen. Now it is our turn to listen, to let him speak to our hearts, and to respond with our hearts.

We may want to go longer, but if we give Jesus even only ten minutes each day to speak to us, to assure us of how much we are loved, cared for, to let us know where we have a sure Source of healing, of comfort, a hope and ultimate meaning, then such daily meetings will transform our lives! As we begin this method of divine reading, the best passages of Scripture to turn to are those of the Gospels. I would especially recommend the Sermon on the Mount (Mt. 5–7) and our Lord's words at the Last Supper (Jn.

13–17). But each will find, again and again, the Lord speaking to him powerfully through different passages. We will want to listen to St. John's wonderful letter of love, or to passages like the message to the Church of Laodicea in the Book of Revelation (3:14–22), the call of Abraham, God's intimacy with Moses, his extravagant love songs (Song of Songs) and wooing (Osee), each in its turn, depending perhaps on where we are in our own spiritual journey, our own love affair with the Lord. Each day, for ten minutes, we will sit down with our divine Friend and let him "open the Scriptures to us" and let his Spirit set our hearts ablaze within us.

At the end of the time we have allotted for our meeting with the Lord, we should thank him. It is really something wonderful, isn't it, that whenever we want, we can call upon the Lord, and he will sit down with us and speak to us. How great is the love of our God!

And as we move on into our continuing activity, we take a word with us. Some days there will be no question what that word should be. He will have spoken a word to us so powerfully that it will abide with us for days, even weeks, months, and years. (As I write this, there comes to my mind a word he spoke to me over twenty years ago—and still at this moment it immediately becomes fire in my heart.) On other days we will have to choose a word ourselves deliberately—for it will seem he has not spoken to us in any special way. And so we will choose one to take with us. For example, we might choose from the passage we just read: "Was not our heart burning within us as he opened the Scriptures for us" or "We had hoped" or "they recognized him in the breaking of the bread," or any other that gives us something to savor, to "chew" on. And as we go about the day or night we will return to this "word" and let it speak to us again and again, until it reveals more and more of its message.

It is a wonderful thing to fall asleep with a "word" in our mind and heart—the gateway to a deep, restful sleep, confident that we rest safely in the loving hands of our Father. And to awake with a word of life in our mind, setting us from the first moment on the uphill road of confidence and hope. And we will have this experience: Oftentimes when, during our reading, the Lord seemed to be absent—no word seemed to burn—later in the day, perhaps as we drive to town or put out the garbage, he is suddenly there. And our heart burns within us.

This, then, is a very simple method:

> (1) We take our Bible, come into Presence, do reverence, and ask for the help of the Holy Spirit, who is dwelling in us.

> (2) We listen to the Lord speak to us through the words of Scripture for ten minutes (or whatever time we decide to give him);

> (3) And then we thank him for being with us, and take a word along with us.

As we do this day by day, the Scripture will indeed be opened to us, and we will recognize the Lord not only in the breaking of the bread but in each stranger—more truly a friend in the Lord—who shares our journey, who walks along with us. All will be Presence, and our hearts will burn within us with the fiery light of a luminous faith.

If it is important that every Christian, every follower of Christ, daily meet the Word in a deeply personal way and let him speak to mind and heart through the life-giving words of his revelation, it is especially so for those of us who are entering into Centering Prayer or any contemplative type of prayer.

In active prayer or discursive meditation our minds and affections are very much involved. We ponder on texts, on the truths of revelation. We call up scenes from our memories or imaginations. Affective responses are evoked. Through these faculties our prayer is easily and immediately related with the other activities of our lives in ways we can readily sense and reflect upon. This is quite satisfying and integrating. At the same time, in the course of our prayer we are hearing the word of faith and our faith is built up on the conceptual and affective level.

In contemplative prayer, thoughts, images, and sensible affections are left behind. The experience of God and the activity of love are taking place at a deeper and more intimate level. Our faith and love are being nourished in a deep and all-pervasive way. We develop a connatural sense, as it were, by which we begin to perceive the presence and activity of God in and through all things and to respond to this loving reality. But there still remains in us as integral human persons a need to grow in faith and faith response on the conceptual and affective level. And there is a constant need to be able to relate the deep experience we are having with the rest of our lives through a growing understanding and experience of faith and love on the other levels of our being.

We need, therefore, to do faith reading, for this affords the Lord the welcoming space and the opportunity—through the exercise of our faith and love, under the movement of his grace and the gifts of the Holy Spirit—to relate to the other levels of our lives the deep, intimate experience of himself that he has been granting us in contemplative prayer. Our contemplative experience, then, feeds directly into our faith-reading, bringing to it a certain fire and light and experiential reality, through which it is able to flow into our lives at the level of affect and concept. The experience of meeting God in sacred reading has an integrating effect.

On a number of occasions, Westerners who have had a prolonged experience in various types of Eastern meditation have shared this with me: They were very faithful to their meditations, and they had many very good experiences within the meditations. They saw certain fruits flowing into their lives from the meditations, at least as far as they could ascribe a causal effect. Yet in their own inner self they were not able to relate their experience in meditation with the rest of their lives. They were not equipped to relate with the everyday realities of their lives their transcendental experience of the Absolute, the No-thingness, or whatever name for the Transcendent was used in their particular discipline.

There was, especially, the problem of love. The transcendental experience was beautiful, but they were not discerning in it the presence of another who could be related to personally and could be loved. And yet, at least from the orientation that lived in them from their Western culture (and I would affirm, from the very reality of things), a loving, affective relationship was perceived as a necessary and integral part of full human happiness and completion. There was a real need for being related to the One they experienced in their meditation, in the love that motivated the whole

flow of their lives. The great Eastern masters were aware of this
need and constantly urged their disciples to integrate their experience into their own religious culture. But, unfortunately, all too
often there was no one in their own religious community who was
able and willing to help them to do this. Indeed, at times they met
with the affirmation that such an integration was not possible. Con-
sequently these meditators found themselves in a very painful situation.

Those participating in Christian contemplation also need to be
able to relate their contemplative experience to the other activities
of their lives. Encountering God in his Word, in the personal revelation of his most loving Self—"I no longer call you servants but
friends because I make known to you all the Father has made
known to me"—enables this deep experience to be fleshed out, as it
were, into something that fully responds to the longing and need of
the human person. At the same time, the contact with God in the
revelation of his goodness creates in the person the desire to return
to the center and have an ever fuller immediate experience of God's
presence and caring love.

As we see, there is a reciprocity. Sacred reading creates a desire
for deeper experience and at the same time is itself brought to fire
by such experience. Contemplative experience creates a thirst for
more knowledge of the Beloved, to be found in his revelation. This
seems to be a hallmark of true Christian experience: it always
creates a greater desire to search the Scriptures, and at the same
time it finds in that conceptual knowledge, with its affective response, the means of expressing itself on the other levels of the
Christian's life.

So when we pass from active, discursive prayer to the practice of
contemplative prayer, faith-reading, sacred reading, the encounter
with God in his Word, becomes much more important and meaningful in our lives. We ought, therefore, to include in our daily program not only two twenty-minute periods of Centering Prayer but
at least ten or fifteen minutes of sacred reading along the lines of
the method we have shared. This might seem to add up to a lot of
time, but it is still a long way from a tithe of our day, of the time
the Lord gratuitously gives to us to use as we will. Can we not,

should we not, give back to God in a very direct and personal way at least a tithe of what he has given us? After our morning and evening meditation, who of us can say that our days are so crowded with essential concerns that we cannot take a ten-minute break with our dearest and most beloved? And if the day is really so taken up, then who of us cannot spare ten minutes of the night? Medieval writers speak of falling asleep with the Sacred Text in their hands, upon their breasts, as they were meditating on the Sacred Word. If we are indeed exhausted from the labors of the day, what better way could we go to sleep, with the almost absolute assurance of waking to prayer, and of the angels hovering over us, bringing our sleep as prayer before the throne of God: "I sleep, but my heart watches" (Sg. 5:2).

A few minutes of sacred reading each day is not only important, it seems virtually essential if we are going to live a centered life, a life wherein the immediate experience of God (which we enjoy in our Centering Prayer) is integrated into the rest of our activities and is able to express itself as a life-giving leaven, as an inner spirit, as fire in the heart.

XII

RELAX!

"Come to me, all you who labor and are heavily burdened, and I will refresh you." Who of us does not at one time or other have a sense of being heavily burdened? Who of us does not labor at the tasks of life and yearn for true refreshment?

The man who made my opening statement is a Jew. As a Jew, he thinks and speaks in a Semitic way. The "you" he speaks of is very concrete and real. It is you and me, and the whole of you and me. It is not some part of us, some spiritual dimension. In prayer the Lord wants to refresh us in our entirety. Being a man, he knows a man's fatigues on every level of his being. In his love he wants to respond to all these needs.

We can readily agree that prayer should be refreshing spiritually. That is to be expected. (But some of the spiritual exercises and complicated methods proposed could lead us to wonder if prayer is not one of the greatest and most fatiguing of labors. This certainly was not our Lord's intent.) He who no longer calls us servants but friends wants prayer to be as refreshing as sitting down to an intimate meal with a beloved friend. Prayer should be spiritually refreshing. And, as we have already seen in our consideration of thoughts, it is also geared to be psychologically refreshing. It should, moreover, be physically renewing and strengthening. When we pray, we are touching the Source of our being, of all our life and vitality, and new creative energies are set loose to flow through us.

Prayer, deep prayer, contemplative prayer, Centering Prayer, has many analogies to sleep. This is true as regards physical refreshment. We know from experience that if we are tense when we retire, tied up in knots, and go to sleep that way, we will wake up not refreshed by our night's repose but more tense and worn. On the other hand, if we retire quite relaxed, we will sleep well and wake up more relaxed and truly refreshed.

So it is with Centering Prayer. If we enter into it feeling taut and tense and do not take a bit of time to relax and let our muscles loosen up, we will come out of the Prayer just as tense as when we went into it, if not more so. And the tenseness will certainly not facilitate our Prayer. But if we enter into it in a relaxed state, we will be deeply refreshed, even physically. Stored-up tensions in our body will seep out. We will have allowed the Lord to do what he wants to do: to refresh us integrally as human persons very dear to him.

Some of us are ordinarily quite relaxed. Usually we have to do no more than get settled in a comfortable position, and whatever strain or tightness we may have picked up in our activities will flow out and we will be relaxed. With other persons, though, that is not the case. It is for the latter that the few suggestions offered in this chapter are primarily intended. However, as a matter of fact, most of us at one time or another may have a little difficulty in trying to settle down when we come to prayer. So maybe all of us can profit from a few simple methods for letting go of some of our bodily tensions in order to free ourselves for prayer.

One of the benefits deriving from taking a minute or two to do a bit of exercise before centering is this: As we turn our attention to the simple exercises, our minds let go of their preoccupations and give themselves to guiding the gentle movements of our bodies. The exercises are not such that they tend to engross us, so when they are over, our minds readily leave them behind and find themselves quite empty and ready to move into the Prayer.

We do not want any big program of exercises. Most people already have some difficulty in making space in a busy life for the

twenty minutes of meditation. To significantly extend this time
would only add to the time strain and perhaps undermine fidelity.
Of course, if we already have a program of exercise, especially
something like Yoga, we can very profitably program our day so
that this immediately precedes our meditation and prepares us for
it, but an extensive program is not needed. Yet it is good to know of
some exercises that we can easily and even quite discreetly do
when our place of meditation does not lend itself to something
more elaborate. For this reason I will share here a few routines, one
or the other of which might suit us better in general or in a particular situation.

Three Deep Breaths

The first we will consider is a very simple breathing exercise.
When we think of breathing exercises in conjunction with meditation, we rather spontaneously think of Yoga. It is certainly true that
some of the Eastern traditions have developed the physical comple-
ments to meditation far more fully than has ever been done in the
West. Yet such practices are not wholly foreign to our Christian tradition. As mentioned earlier in this book, in the medieval development of the tradition of the Jesus Prayer or the Prayer of the Heart
among our Orthodox brothers, we find extensive use of psychosomatic elements, including the breath. In the presently quite popular spiritual classic *The Way of the Pilgrim,* the author considers
this rather precisely. Centering Prayer, however, is a very simple
and pure method. In its actual practice we completely disregard
the breath. But it is possible to turn our attention to it for a few
moments when preparing to enter into our Prayer.

For this first exercise, we want to get settled comfortably in the
position we will continue to hold when we go on to meditate. As
mentioned in a previous chapter, for most of us in the West the
best posture for prayer is to settle down in a chair, one that will
support our back and keep it quite straight. When our spine is
straight, each bone can rest comfortably on top of the one below
without any strain, and the head, which is actually quite heavy pro-
portionately, can be well supported. If the chair is adequately sup-

portive, we can let go completely and allow our body to rest in the chair, with muscles wholly relaxed.

To facilitate this complete relaxation, after gently closing our eyes (the eyelids should not be pressed together or clamped shut, but just gently resting over the eyes), we allow all the air that is in our lungs to seep out gently, contracting the stomach. We should not use force, but just sense that we have "emptied out" all the stale air. Then we inhale deeply, expanding the stomach (before we begin, we should be sure that our clothing is sufficiently loose), and let in a flood of good fresh air, full of oxygen. We hold this for a moment—not with discomfort, but just to let everything in us be completely still for a few moments and to allow our system to absorb the oxygen. Then we gently contract the stomach and allow all the air to flow out again. This very simple inhalation and exhalation is repeated two more times, each time allowing a few moments of stability when the lungs are filled. Then we enter into the first step of our Centering Prayer, turning our attention to the Presence.

Most people are surprised, the first time they try this, to discover what a difference this simple exercise makes. The mind is free and empty, sensing a greater clarity and repose, ready to rest in the Lord. The rhythm of our whole body, and not just of our breathing, has slowed down, quieted, and is supportive of our finding the deep quiet within. This is, as you can see, a very simple exercise, and one that can be done even in a public place without attracting notice.

Rolling the Head

This second exercise is also quite simple, but more effective, though it might attract attention if we were to do it sitting in a plane or in some other public place. After getting settled in our chair and closing our eyes, we gently expel all the stale air from our lungs by contracting the diaphragm. But, this time, as we expel the air, we allow our head to fall down on our chest. Then as we draw in the fresh air we raise our head—every movement is made slowly and gently—and let it fall back as far as it will, or as far as our chair will allow. After a slight repose, we repeat the exercise and do it twice more.

We may stop there and enter into our meditation. However, if we wish to do a bit more, we may continue with three more breaths. But, this time, instead of raising the head and letting it fall back, we roll it around to the right till it settles in the back. After the repose, as we exhale, we continue to roll the head around till it again settles on our chest and all the air is expelled from our lungs. This, too, can be done three times.

This exercise adds to the first a loosening of the muscles around the neck and shoulders—a loosening that tends to flow to the rest of the body, taking the frown from our forehead, the tightness from the crown of our head, and letting the tenseness flow down from the trunk and the extremities, to empty out through the tips of our fingers and toes. Again, a very simple exercise with a surprisingly extensive effect.

Controlled Bodily Relaxation

This next exercise, Father William Meninger calls "controlled bodily relaxation." He takes his listeners through it in one of his excellent cassette recordings on contemplative prayer. Doing it with a leader like Father William is certainly a great advantage, but we can also guide ourselves through it. We begin, again, by assuming that posture which is proper for our centering. We then focus our attention on the left foot. We imagine it as being totally relaxed and at ease. We sense all the tension flowing out of it. When we feel it is fully relaxed, we move on to the ankle. Again, focusing our attention, we imagine the ankle is being fully relaxed and at ease, all the tension flowing out. As we sense each part becoming fully relaxed, we move on to the next. First up the left side: foot, ankle, calf, knee, thigh; then up the right; then the hips, the stomach, and even the inner organs if we are able.

We then go to the lower back and move up methodically, coming to the shoulder blades, first the left, then the right. We go around to the front again, to the chest: first the left side, then the right; then the shoulders—left, right—allowing them to slump a bit if they will. From the shoulders we move down the arms, first the left, then the right: upper arm, elbow, forearm, hand, sensing all the tension flowing out the tips of our fingers.

Next we turn our attention to the neck, and let it relax all around; then our jaws, the tongue, the root of the tongue down in the throat. All the muscles around the lips; we sense the tension flowing out and everything relaxing. Then the left cheekbone, the right, the muscles under each eye, the eyelids—often an area of great tension—and the eyebrows. We let the tension flow out of our furrowed brow—relax, relax, relax. Then the scalp, the skin and muscles in the back of our head; we focus our attention successively on each area, sense the tension flowing out, allow the part to fully relax, and move on to the next.

This exercise actually does not take a great deal of time, yet it leads to very deep and complete relaxation. It can be combined with the three breaths; in fact, that is what Father William does in his cassette talks; yet this is not necessary. Like the breathing exercise, it can be done anywhere without attracting any attention.

Total-relaxation Exercise

The last exercise I will share with you is one of my favorites. It is a lot of fun when you do it together before a group meditation. But it calls for a bit of space and is not something you would want to start doing in an airport (unless you are a complete extrovert and like to attract lots of attention).

This exercise is done standing up. First we raise our right hand above our head and reach for the ceiling—or the sky, if the ceiling is too low. We really stretch, a little more than we think we can. We press our limits just a little. After holding this stretch for a few moments, we allow the arm to fall gently to the side and repeat the stretch with the left arm, as far as we can, and then a little more. Hold it! and then let the left arm fall gently to the side.

Next we allow our head to fall forward, our arms dangling, our body bending at the waist. We do not worry about keeping the knees straight. We are completely relaxed, letting our head fall as far as it will—even to the floor! We rest in this deep body bend for a bit and then gently resume an upright position.

Now we place our feet together and raise both arms till they are fully extended, parallel to the shoulders, forming a cross. Without moving our feet, we gently twist our body to the right as far as we can—and then a bit more—and more. After holding the furthermost twist for a few moments, we reverse our direction and twist as far as we can to the left—and then some, and then hold it for a bit before returning to the center, relaxing, and letting our arms fall to our sides.

Keeping our feet together, we now place our right hand under our chin (if we have a beard we might just grab it) and place our left hand on the back of our head. We gently twist our head as far as we can to the right—and again a little more (no one has yet twisted his head off, as far as I know). After holding the twist for a bit, we relax, return to the center, switch hands, and twist off to the left. By the time we return to the center and drop our arms gently to our sides we will have stretched every muscle in our body. And if we have pressed just a little "beyond our limit," we will feel very good. We can now sink down into our meditation chair and enter very peacefully into our center.

These are all very simple exercises. There is nothing spectacular or even unusual about them. They work. They are enough to dissipate bodily tension, empty the mind, and dispose us for a meditation within which the Lord can refresh us in the way he wills.

None of these exercises, and certainly not all of them, should be considered a part of our Centering Prayer. They can be done very prayerfully. They can indeed be prayer, bodily worship. But they are simply offered by way of option. In some cases, one might suggest their use, even recommend it. Yet they are ad lib. The important thing is to relax as we enter into the Prayer. How each one does that is completely up to him or her. Our body should be disposed to facilitate the quieting of the spirit and to receive the refreshment the Lord wants to give. But each of us should feel totally free to find the way that is most suitable for him or her to bring about a receptive state of relaxation.

XIII

SOME QUESTIONS AND ANSWERS

One of the reasons why I like to teach Centering Prayer and lead
Centering Prayer workshops is that as I teach others I always learn
more myself. The learner is looking to me with expectation—an expectation that is certainly not based on anything I have, but on a
confident hope that God will speak through this brother in Christ.
To such a confidence God cannot fail to respond. The message of
presence and love that he speaks to each is absolutely unique, for
he speaks to each one precisely according to who he or she is and
where he or she is. The message, then, is new and different each
time. And as the Lord gives this to me for his expectant disciple, I
myself perceive new aspects that I had not seen before. In each
workshop, in each teaching session, new elements are highlighted
and different aspects are brought together in new ways, shedding
light on each other. This especially takes place as I try to respond
to the questions that are asked.

In the hope of shedding more light on the teaching we have already shared, I would like to present here some of the more common questions that are asked and try to respond to them.

Is Centering Prayer for Everyone?

I think we have to distinguish between what Centering Prayer is
essentially, and Centering Prayer as a particular method to enter

into that experience. Every Christian, by his very nature as a baptized child of God, is meant to have a deep, loving relationship with God that will go beyond words and concepts, thoughts and feelings. But there are many ways by which one can grow in this relationship and come to this experience of God's presence and love.

The Rosary is a wonderful school of prayer which has led many Catholics into the deepest kind of union with God. I know a wonderful woman whose whole life has been one of love, of giving herself to everyone in love: her family, friends, anyone she hears of who is in need. Now that she is getting on in years, when her service is not immediately needed and she is a bit too worn to go out seeking to serve, she sits by her window, across the street from a hospital, and prays the Rosary for the world she looks out upon. She never formulated the ideal of contemplative prayer for herself. She wonders sometimes why it takes her so long to get through a Rosary. A whole day can pass and the five decades will not be completed. If I told her that much of her time is actually being spent in contemplative prayer, she would probably smile at me sweetly and think I really didn't know what I was talking about.

The Lord leads us each in his or her own way. If one is drawn to investigate Centering Prayer and to begin to use it, it is only by the leading of God's grace, for it is a value beyond what we can perceive by natural reason. And such a grace is an invitation from the Lord to enter into the ways of contemplative prayer. I do not think we should hesitate to share Centering Prayer with anyone who seeks to learn about it or whose life indicates that he or she is trying to pray and get in closer touch with God.

How does this square with the teaching, which seems to be quite common, that one needs to be grounded through a long practice of active prayer before one is ready for contemplative prayer?

A century ago, the prevailing practice, which had been in vogue in the West for many centuries and is still holding in the East, insisted that one should receive the Holy Eucharist infrequently and only after a long and serious preparation. Those who encouraged frequent Communion were thought to be irreverent, to be lacking in a full understanding of what was involved, to be out of step with true Catholic tradition. Fortunately, the latter's truer understanding of God's tremendous love and mercy and his desire for intimacy prevailed. At the turn of the century, one of these latter became pope, a saintly pope, Pope St. Pius X. He showed the Catholic community that this prevailing tradition was a late one and led the Church back to the truer, early tradition, and opened frequent Communion to all. His successors have followed in his spirit and have done everything possible to remove all obstacles and to encourage all to receive Holy Communion every time they participate in the celebration of the Liturgy.

Abbot Thomas Keating, in an excellent chapter in the book *Finding Grace at the Center* (see Bibliography), has shown how the Western Christian community has lost an important part of its heritage in relegating the contemplative experience to the preserve of a few advanced souls. Our concern in fostering Centering Prayer has been to help Western Christians to recover the earlier and truer tradition which invited all to a very simple practice of prayer that is open to the contemplative experience. The experience of God is a gift of God. But ordinarily we have to make room in our lives for this gift in response to hearing his Word of Love. Centering Prayer is an early traditional method—in a new packaging—for doing this. There is no better way to express our love for God and our desire that he manifest himself to us and bring us into this intimate experience of himself in love, than by consistently making space for him in our life with longing love and quieted mind.

But are there some who cannot do Centering Prayer?

I think we have to say, "Yes," to that. All prayer is a gift. God does not give the gift of this kind of prayer to all. If one is not attracted to this kind of prayer it may be simply because he or she is not receiving the grace to see its value. It is not for that person at this time. It may become so later on, or God may continue always to lead that person in another way. The important thing is that each one respond to the Lord's leadings, and pray and give time regularly to serious prayer.

To pray, one must really want God, want a relationship with him. Without such a desire—it need not be a felt desire; it may be just a "cold" decision of the will in response to perceived reality—one cannot enter into Centering Prayer or any other kind of prayer.

As we continue in prayer, especially prayer like Centering Prayer, there will arise before our mind's eye, one after the other, all the persons and things we love and are attached to. And as he asked Peter on the shores of the Sea of Galilee, the Lord will ask us: "Do you love me more than these?" If we are to continue in the Prayer, we will have to let go continually. It can involve a great struggle at times. If in the end we do refuse to let go and choose God, we cannot continue in prayer. We have made someone or something else our god.

Father Eugene Boylan, a wonderful spiritual father who has written some excellent books on prayer and the spiritual life, used to say this to his retreatants: "If you will spend fifteen minutes a day in intimate converse with the Lord, really listening to him, I guarantee you will become a saint." I am sure Father Eugene is right. We cannot regularly meet our Lord and continue in any deliberate sin. One or the other will go: the sin or the daily meeting with our Lord. And we cannot regularly meet with anyone as lovable as our Lord and not grow in love. The fifteen minutes will gradually expand until they embrace the whole of our lives.

Grace has its times and its seasons. And we want to move with it. If one is experiencing the first wonderful breathings of the Spirit in an enthusiastic affective charismatic prayer, it is not the time, perhaps, to sit quietly and try to center. That will probably come later. For the moment, love needs to pour itself out in praise and song, in hand clapping and dance, in pure exuberant celebration. Praise the Lord!

Centering Prayer draws its teaching from The Cloud of Unknowing. *But the author of* The Cloud *seems to hedge his teaching around*

*with many precautions as to who should receive this instruction and
practice this contemplative way.*

There are some things I think we need to note about *The Cloud
of Unknowing*. First of all, it is the treatise of a spiritual father
written for his spiritual son, a relatively young man, whom he has
personally instructed at length. That personal instruction is presup-
posed. The text is meant to be a reminder of it, to fill it out, perhaps, but not to be in itself a complete teaching on the spiritual
life. The author realized and intended that his treatise would be
shared by others. Yet, like all conscientious spiritual fathers, he was
a man of great prudence and caution. He realized the dangers of
Quietism—an error that would soon become rampant in the Church
—and spiritual pride. In reading about a lofty spiritual ideal, there
is always danger one might begin to strive for it without listening
to the promptings of the inner Spirit. Moreover, this spiritual father
was very sensitive. He did not want to be responsible before God
for leading persons whom he himself or some other spiritual father
had not adequately tested. We should respect such a man.

We need to be conscious, too, of the fact that he was a man of
another time, writing for a man of his own time. We will often find
his style unfamiliar if not difficult. This should warn us that we cannot readily grasp his teaching and put it into practice with the
same straightforward literalness we would a contemporary teaching
on prayer. We have attempted to present something of his teaching
in a new package precisely to be of some help in making it available today.

In his closing chapter, the author does make it quite clear whom
he considers ready to receive his instruction on contemplative
prayer. A person is ready for contemplative prayer when he has left
off all deliberate sin, or at least has brought all such sin to the
Church for healing and has a firm purpose of amendment (see Ch.
28), is drawn to a simple prayer, and is not really at peace except
when he knows he is seeking God's will in all things. The author
does not insist that such feelings prevail "continually and perma-
nently right from the beginning, for such is not the case." The fact
that one has perhaps been quite deviant and still feels alien attrac-

tions and desires, has weaknesses and failings, does not rule out a present call to contemplation: "It is not what you are nor what you have been that God sees with his all-merciful eyes, but what you desire to be." If one has a simple desire to be deeply united to God, to experience his love and respond to it, "he need have no fear of error in believing that God is calling him to contemplation, regardless of what sort of person he is now or has been in the past." When properly understood, the author of *The Cloud* does not attach the call to contemplation to any specially lofty or advanced stage of holiness. One needs but to have actually turned from deliberate sin and to be desirous of a simple union with God in prayer.

But what of the well-known criteria of St. John of the Cross concerning the call to contemplative prayer?

Father William Johnston, in his edition of *The Cloud of Unknowing*, has highlighted the congruence between the teaching of the author of *The Cloud* and the Spanish Doctor of Prayer. That the latter depended on the former, or at least was familiar with his work, is not established, but they certainly shared a common tradition. The criteria of St. John are not really different from those of *The Cloud,* but they are expressed and developed more fully, as is his whole teaching on prayer. He delineates his signs most concisely in the thirteenth chapter of the second book of *The Ascent of Mount Carmel:*

> The first is the realization that one cannot make discursive meditation nor receive any satisfaction from it. . . .
>
> The second sign is an awareness of a disinclination to fix the imagination or sense faculties upon other particular objects, exterior or interior. I am not affirming that the imagination will cease to come and go (even in deep recollection it usually wanders freely), but that the person is disinclined to fix it purposely upon extraneous things.
>
> The third and surest sign is that a person likes to remain in loving awareness of God, without particular consideration, in interior peace and quiet and repose, and without the acts and exercises (at

least discursive, those in which one progresses from point to point) of the intellect, memory and will; and that he prefers to remain only in the general, loving awareness and knowledge we mentioned, without any particular knowledge or understanding.

Again, we have to be aware that our author is a man of another time, writing for the men and women of his period. It was a time when a rationalist approach prevailed in society and in the study of theology, and carried over into the practice of prayer. One was quite content to engage in interior discourse and imaginative developments concerning the facts of revelation and the truths of theology. It was only by a grace from God that a person could be weaned away from the intellectual activity and drawn to a desire to rest in the Lord in the Reality beyond thought.

In our times, nature readily aids grace in this. It is a time when experience is given preference over conceptual knowledge and intellectual understanding. Right from the very beginning, many experience an inability to pursue discursive meditation or find any satisfaction in it. There is no desire to remain in the realm of one's own imagination. Rather, one very quickly comes to desire to remain in immediate loving experiential awareness of God in peace and quiet and repose.

St. John himself does say that when one prays regularly one is drawn to contemplative prayer quite soon. He does not specify precisely what "quite soon" means, but I think today it is sooner than ever before.

Why not use one's mind and one's thoughts to communicate with God? Why shouldn't prayer use the same sort of state of consciousness as is used the rest of the day?

Certainly we should use our minds and our thoughts in communicating with God. We are commanded to pray without ceasing. As we go through the day, we will engage in many kinds of prayer and amply use our minds and thoughts if we are going to fulfill this divine command. Even Centering Prayer in its initial movement uses mind and thought, heart and affection. But what we are seeking in Centering Prayer is, at least for a few minutes a day, to go beyond our own minds and thoughts. Even in our everyday experience, when we love someone in a special way we sense the need to have moments alone with that person, to be quiet and to communicate on deeper levels than words and thoughts can convey. If this is true in ordinary human relations, how much greater a need is there of this when the person with whom we are communicating in actual fact completely transcends all thought, all that our minds can ever grasp?

What is the difference between this kind of quiet prayer and Quietism, which was a heresy condemned by the Church?

Quietism is the name given to a spiritual doctrine which, as proposed by Miguel de Molinos, was condemned in 1687. This teaching maintained that one can bring about passive contemplation, or the mystical activity of God in the soul, at will, simply by ceasing every operation of the faculties. Setting this up as the ideal, it repudiated all conscious activity as an infidelity to grace. This was extended to the whole of life and even condemned an examination of one's acts. From this it made the leap to holding that exterior acts that were objectively sinful were not morally reprehensible if they did not interfere with one's interior quiet. In making the cessation of all human activity and inner quiet the ideal, this pseudo spirituality approached the ideal of some of the Eastern practices and departed from the primacy of love, which marks all Christian life and activity.

Centering Prayer is, as the author of *The Cloud* constantly states, a work of love. The whole of the Prayer is actually contained in the first step, attending in faith and love to God present at the center, or ground, of our being. The rest of the method is meant but to enable us to abide as wholly and purely as possible in this act of love. The prayer word is meaningful in that it expresses that love and resumes in greatest simplicity the whole of our love relationship.

The difference, then, between this prayer of quiet and Quietism is evident: the former is a continuous act of love, the latter seeks the cessation of all such acts. The former seeks to animate all our activity outside of the time of prayer with the activity of love; the latter seeks to void all exterior acts of any interior activity. The former aims at bringing one fully into act as a human person; the latter would have the human person become a totally passive entity that is only acted upon. While a superficial glance might see a likeness between the two, in essence they could hardly be more unlike.

Is this also how Centering Prayer differs from TM? I have heard some say that Centering Prayer is only a baptized TM.

What we have said about the way Quietism differs from Centering Prayer does indeed apply in part also to TM (Transcendental Meditation), if one is speaking only about the basic meditation technique. The Siddhis program more recently propagated by Maharishi Mahesh Yogi is quite an active practice. The basic meditation practice does have an affinity to Quietism. It seeks inner quiet rather than fostering an active love relationship with God. However, it is unlike Quietism and more like Centering Prayer in that it does hope to animate the rest of one's life and even the whole of creation by the meditation experience. However, the TM technique, while it has some apparent similarities to Centering Prayer, is essentially different and works from different principles. Instead of using a meaningful prayer word that involves an affective response, it employs a meaningless sound, and this is to be used throughout the time of meditation instead of only when it is needed to return to Presence. The purpose for which one does TM is usually not religious. The practice itself is simply a natural human activity by which one seeks to put himself in touch with the ground of his being. But, like all human acts, it can be invested with religious significance. Hindus have employed it, giving their own particular meaning to it. And Christians can use it, filling it out with the fuller understanding supplied by revelation.

Pope John Paul II spoke of this recently when he said: "Being faithful to the genuine and total message of the Lord, it is necessary for the Church to open and to interpret all human reality in order to impregnate it with the strength of the Gospel" (Cuilápan, Mexico, Jan. 29, 1979: *Origins*, 8:543).

Christ isn't just a guru of a spiritual way. Isn't there a danger, in approaching prayer this way, of losing sight of some of the values of Christianity?

If this were the only way a person prayed, and if he made this prayer the whole of his spiritual life—yes, indeed! But it is proposed that one devote only two or three short periods in the day to this kind of prayer. These periods will be times of intense love, refreshing moments of experiencing God's presence and love, which will animate the rest of the activities of the day and especially the other forms of prayer: the celebration of the sacraments and the Eucharist, and communing with the Lord in Holy Scripture. These latter, in their turn, will increase our desire for this work of love. Centering Prayer is meant to be practiced in the context of a total Christian life and to bear fruit in it.

Where is Christ in Centering Prayer? I want to pray as a Christian.

Centering Prayer aims at enabling us not only to pray as Christians but to pray as Christ. We are Christ in virtue of our baptism: "I live, now not I, but Christ lives in me" (Ga. 2:20). And we have been given Christ's Spirit as our Spirit: "We do not know how to pray as we ought, but the Holy Spirit has been poured out in our hearts and cries, 'Abba—Father'" (cf. Ga. 4:6). In Centering Prayer we let go of our own thoughts and feelings and join our hearts, our wills, with Christ's. We let his Spirit, who is now also our Spirit, pray within us. Christ is more intimately present in our prayer than we are ourselves. A prayer could not be more Christian.

This sounds a little pantheistic to me. I am me—a poor sinful creature, and Christ is God!

Our Lord said: "One is good—God" (Mk. 10:18). All that is, is good; indeed, all that is, is God. God *is:* "I Am who I Am" (Ex. 3:14). God is all goodness, all beauty, all being. Everything and everyone that has goodness, beauty, being, has it only in so far as he, she, or it is a participation of God. This is profoundly mysterious. When we get in touch with the ground of our being, we in some way experience this oneness with God, who is. We know that in some way we remain distinct from God, but it is difficult, if not impossible, to keep hold of this in the midst of the experience.

The Fathers and mystics of the Church have constantly spoken of a coming into unity with God: a divine union, a transforming union, a unity of spirit. Without the help of the historical revelation, our brothers in other religions in their struggle to convey their experience have come up with articulations that are or sound pantheistic. Some Christian writers—men such as Tauler and Suso—have been accused of the same.

We are struggling to express the inexpressible. We are certainly distinct from God. We are poor sinners. And yet we are one with God, sharing in his being and goodness, for he is all that is. And we, by baptism, have been brought into an even fuller sharing and oneness with him in Christ. It is all true and we can deny none of it. Yet we can hardly put it all together. As we speak, we necessarily speak at one time of one aspect of this total reality and at another time of another aspect. We cannot say everything at the same time, but we have to be understood as speaking in the context of the whole of the mystery.

What about the Cross? Isn't it central to Christianity and Christian prayer? Centering Prayer is so simple, peaceful, and restful—isn't the Cross being left out?

If anyone thinks that Centering Prayer leaves out the Cross, he or she need only practice this Prayer faithfully over a period of time. It is easy, it is simple—but it is also relentless in its demands.

The first great demand it makes is to ask for some of our precious time twice a day—a real asceticism in the midst of our busy days. There are so many other things we could be doing for God! Our self-importance as God's necessary agents has to be significantly deflated. Our passionate desire to be a doer, to get things done, to assure ourselves of our worth by our accomplishments, by others' dependence on us—all this has to be significantly disciplined to enable us to be free to let everything go regularly at the height of our day and sit quietly with the Lord for twenty minutes; to enable us to retire early enough so as to be able to rise sufficiently early to give the Lord this time before we sweep into the day's activities. And there is that very down-to-earth asceticism of getting our feet out from under the covers and down to earth when the alarm clock rudely announces it is time to rise and pray.

Once we accomplish this necessary prerequisite and humbly and perhaps heroically make the time to sit down with the Lord, there is within the very practice of the Prayer a demand for a courageous dying to self. The very simplicity of the Prayer we find difficult. We like things that are complicated, hard, that demand a certain genius, so that in their accomplishment we can pat ourselves on the back for our great achievement. We love to complicate things so that we can congratulate ourselves on our ability in figuring them out. But in this Prayer, where all we do is let go and let God do, there isn't much room left for back-patting.

If Centering Prayer is simple, and in that sense easy, it is in its very simplicity quite ruthless. To be faithful to the Prayer, we must let go of *everything:* all our beautiful—and not so beautiful but sometimes very enticing—thoughts and feelings, all our rich images, all those wonderful inspirations that come along; the solutions that pop up to the questions and problems we have been struggling with, the perfect idea, text, phrase, or program—*everything*—and above all, even our very selves.

Whenever anything of self grabs for our attention, we are simply to let go and turn, by means of our prayer word, to the present God —centering our whole attention on him.

There is a very real dying to self here—a real *mortification,* a "making dead." When somebody opposes us, fights us, even curses us, he at least affirms by his action that we do exist. But when someone simply and completely ignores us, he really does us in. We are reduced, as far as he is concerned, to nonentity. We simply do not exist. In Centering Prayer, self, with all its doings, is simply ignored. Each time it does succeed in diverting our attention to itself, we simply let go and return wholly to the Lord.

No exceptions! Each and every time we become aware of anything save our Present Lord, we let it go immediately, but oh so gently; no fight, no struggle, just a gentle *turning to*—not *from;* we do not give the object that much attention—a gentle turning back to the Lord. Simple? Yes! Demanding? Very! Let those who fear that Centering Prayer might be too easy—leaving out the Cross, bypassing death-to-self, asceticism, mortification—just attempt to practice it faithfully!

But we do not follow our Divine Master up the Mount, making time for Centering Prayer, and let ourselves be raised up with him on his saving Cross—being drawn into the cloud of unknowing—to stay there. Calvary is not the center of the great basilica in Jerusalem. In fact the Hill of the Skull is oddly tucked in a corner. The center is the empty Tomb and the glorious sanctuary. Our aim in prayer and in life is to enter into and live more fully that glorified life which is truly ours. We have been baptized into the death and life of the Lord. We have come up out of the water. The risen life is already ours. This is what Centering Prayer emphasizes. The death, the dying-to-self, the making-dead—mortification—is there, but we want to pass through it, go beyond it with Christ and enter into the living experience of our risen life in him who has taken his seat at the right hand of the Father and compassionately lavishes his good gifts upon his people.

Isn't there a danger, if we leave off thinking and judging and just be quiet, that we might be opening not to God and his activity but to the activity of the evil spirits?

St. John of the Cross brings out in his teaching that when we enter into contemplative prayer, we need have no fear of the deceptions of the Evil One, because he cannot touch us at that level of our being. He can only affect those images and feelings that are influenced through the body. He cannot himself penetrate into our spiritual being. There is danger, a need for discernment, in active prayer, in which we are using our imagination and feelings, for he can influence these. But in Centering Prayer we ignore these faculties and simply let images and feelings float away. They do not affect our prayer, so the Evil One cannot touch it. We are engaged at a level that the Lord has made his own through grace and baptism. We are out of the Devil's reach. Only God can penetrate this level of our being. So we are completely safe in contemplative prayer.

What do we do with the burden of sin that comes up? Experiencing our solidarity with others, we realize how unjust, violent, evil, selfish we have been. Sometimes the sense of our sinfulness is overwhelming.

In the course of our Prayer, no matter what feelings, what sensations, what insights arise, we should simply follow the third rule and gently return to the Lord by the use of our prayer word. This is not the time when our Lord wants us to work at these things. At the moment, he is concerned with freeing us from the tension and strain they are causing in us. There is a time and place for facing our sin and guilt, and working with them. Such a time might be when we are making our examen or when we are sitting down with our spiritual father or mother or friend. At such a time, we might want to center for a bit to allow these things to arise again, with all their pain, and at the same time to get in touch with the Source of all strength and consolation so we can be strengthened to face what we have to deal with.

If at other times, outside our prayer, we are plagued by a sense of guilt or any other disturbing or unwanted feeling or thought, our Centering Prayer can come to our rescue, especially if we have gained a certain facility in the use of the Prayer. Instead of trying to fight off the unwanted thought or feeling, and perhaps strengthening its hold by the struggle, we can instead simply use our prayer word to go for a moment to the center and let the thought or feeling float away while we touch ground and are renewed by the ever-present Creative Love.

There is a time for facing our burden of sin and guilt, but even this should not be overdone. In his first sermon on the Song of Songs, St. Bernard of Clairvaux has some wise counsel. Using the image of embracing the feet of the Lord, he tells us that one foot is the foot of justice and the other, the foot of mercy. If we embrace the foot of justice too long, we are overwhelmed by our sin and misery and are in danger of despair. On the other hand, if we embrace the foot of mercy too long we are apt to become overly lax. We need to embrace the one at one time, and the other at another, in a healthy alternation.

How does the inactivity of contemplative prayer prepare us for the activity of everyday life besides fulfilling its function as a time of mental, emotional, and physical rest?

I think this question has been answered for the most part in the chapter on the effects of Centering Prayer in our lives. The experience of God's love for us and of our own lovableness and worth frees us from our defensiveness and allows us to go out to others, to affirm them, to bring to them what we have received from the Lord. Deep prayer opens the way for the fruits of the Spirit to grow in our life: love, joy, peace, kindness, benignity and chastity—attitudes and virtues that will greatly help us in our daily living out of our Christian life in the service of others and of our God.

We hear a lot today about liberation and liberation theology. Can you connect Centering Prayer with this?

To be a liberator, one has himself to be a free person. We have just spoken about how this Prayer frees us from our defensiveness and also from the need to project and submit to the mask of a false self.

It has been said that the Gospels are summed up in the Sermon on the Mount, and the Sermon on the Mount is summed up in the Beatitudes. Indeed, we have in the Beatitudes a whole program of Christian life. The very first of them is the kernel of the Good News: "Blessed are the poor in spirit for theirs is the kingdom"—not at some future time, but already now—the verb is in the present tense. Poverty of spirit is freedom not only from having but from wanting to have. It is a word of goodness that even the poor need to hear. It is perhaps they who most need to hear this word of liberation from the oppression of their wants. But who can proclaim such a word except he who is himself truly free? Such true poverty is known and experienced only when one has stood in his center in his true being in God. Centering Prayer will free us and enable us to speak the word of true freedom to others.

Intercessory prayer is very important to me, but how can I pray for others while I am centering?

I recently heard a story that touched me rather deeply. It was told by a Baptist minister, Dr. Glenn Hinson. He had taken his class of divinity students to Gethsemani Abbey for a visit. Father Louis (Thomas Merton), a name unfamiliar to them, was assigned to show them around and answer their questions. At the end of the meeting one of the students asked Father: "What is a smart guy like you doing holed up in a place like this?" Father Merton replied: "I believe in the power of intercessory prayer."

I believe every contemplative would say the same. Realizing how at every moment everything is coming forth from the ever-active creative love of God, he is in touch with the awesome mystery that God has willed that his creative activity be in accord with the petitions of his children. Such is the tremendous power and responsibility of our prayer. Just as he made our initial coming into being dependent on the free decision of two of his creatures, so he wills that the evolution of the being of each one of us and of all of us should be dependent on the prayers of all.

When God hears prayer, he does not listen to our lips; he looks to our hearts. For our sake, the two Marys in the Gospel verbalized their concerns: "They have no wine." "He whom you love is sick." But they did not formulate petitions. If some person asks us to pray for him and we rattle off some words in his behalf, little will happen. That is probably why some petitionary prayer does not seem to have any effect. But if we take the concern into our heart, when next we approach the Lord in prayer he will see it there, even if we forget to speak to him about it. And in his love he will attend to it. When we enter into intimate and loving union with the Lord in Centering Prayer, he sees all the concerns of our hearts and takes care of them without our having to say a word about them. If at other times we do formulate petitions, it is not so much that God needs this—not he who reads hearts and knows the deepest things in us—but it helps us to deepen and sustain our concern and to increase our confidence in him.

Is it all right to meditate more than twice a day?

Many people, perhaps most, find it hard enough to make time in their busy days for two meditations, but more and more I find those who are getting in a third. In many cultures there is the very sane practice of the siesta. Busy people in our environment are finding that a short meditation after lunch is a real boost and a great aid for getting through the afternoon with the quality of life and response they desire. Some find that their days begin to be spotted with brief moments of centering; at times of quietness, while waiting or moving about, their prayer word comes to summon them to a moment that truly refreshes.

Our centering should fit into the whole context of our Christian lives. Besides the inroads it can make on our limited time, too much meditation can leave us "spacy" and unable to attend to our activities with the sharpness we should bring to them. There should be a harmony between the time of our contemplative revitalization and our active expansion.

Are there certain times of the day that are better for centering? Are there times when we should not center?

The early morning seems by far the best time for Centering Prayer. We are quiet and rested after our night's sleep, and the whole of creation is in quietness. As soon as we rise and get washed, we might settle into our meditation. Some prefer to do their exercises or jogging first; others, some spiritual or Scriptural reading. That might be good too. But certainly we would want to make our meditation before eating. Another good time is in the early evening, before dinner. We are just a bit tired and our system tends to quiet down. The day also is quieting as evening comes on. Others will find suitable times that will fit in with their respective rhythms of life. We can in fact do Centering Prayer at any time. But one of the least advantageous times seems to be right after eating, especially if we have had a big meal. Our center is somewhere else and our metabolism is up. But if this is the only time we can possibly find to center, it is better to do it then than not to do it at all.

Should we always meditate for exactly twenty minutes? Could we go for a longer period if we felt like it?

"Where the Spirit is, there is freedom." Eastern methods are sometimes quite rigid in their rules. This seems necessary, for they are depending wholly on the method and the human activity. The Christian is always depending primarily on the activity of God. And God is preeminently free. If we are drawn on a particular occasion to spend a longer time in meditation, we should certainly respond to such a prompting of the Spirit. Saying that, I would add a few thoughts.

Most meditators seem to find rather quickly what is the most apt duration for them, and for most that is twenty minutes. A few find that fifteen minutes or so responds to their needs. Others, especially religious and others for whom prayer is a large part of their lives, often find themselves settling into longer periods.

There comes to mind a mother general who took part in the first workshop I conducted for major religious superiors. We had decided to meet every other month for follow-ups. At the first of these meetings, Mother reported that she had not done too well; it was hard to find the time. Others reported the same. At the second meeting, Mother shared a discovery she had made. She realized that the sisters at the motherhouse did not have any more pressing need to see her right after Mass each morning than did the sisters in the other houses, so she began slipping up to her room and centering. She hardly missed a day. At the next meeting, she reported that not only had she not missed a single meditation, but that they were getting longer and longer. Mother finally found her pace, meditating a full hour each time. And much to her surprise, she discovered that even while giving this added time to prayer, she was getting more done than ever.

We have noted how tensions surface during our meditations. This is one reason for limiting the time. We do not want too much to come up at one time. This is not apt to happen unless we indulge in very long meditations. In teaching the young especially, or anyone who is apt to be overly enthusiastic, we should be rather strict in limiting the time. Another reason for guarding a reasonable limit in regard to the duration of our centering is that we want the Prayer to blend into the rhythm of our lives. Prolonged meditations might quiet down our system more than is compatible with the activity that is going to have to follow immediately upon our Prayer. We should respect our physiological makeup. All things have their due proportion, even the expressions of love; love alone can be without measure. God can bring about in us all that he wishes in the least moment, if he so wishes; we do not have to prolong the time to get him to do more, except when he wants it.

How do we know when our time is up?

When we first begin Centering Prayer, that is a question. What we can do in practice is keep a watch or clock where it can be easily seen. Each time the question surfaces, if we are not sure if it is time, we take a look. If it is not time to finish, we gently return to the center with our prayer word. If it is time, we gently close our eyes again and begin the Our Father. If we meditate consistently for the same length of time, we will soon enough find that we automatically know when it is time to end our centering. It is not advisable to set an alarm or a timer that will abruptly draw us out of meditation. It would be better to go overtime than to have such a rude interruption. I have not yet found anyone who has gotten lost in the Prayer for an unduly long time.

What if I find I am falling asleep?

The author of *The Cloud of Unknowing* has a consoling word for us here. He says if we fall asleep during the Prayer, we should not be concerned. Our Father loves us as much when we are asleep as when we are awake. And this is certainly true. If we are going to turn our full attention on the Lord in this Prayer, we cannot be keeping an eye on ourselves to make sure we are not falling asleep. But I would add this: If we find we are falling asleep every time we sit down to center, there may be a message in it for us. It may be that we are getting too comfortable. The body is getting the message that it is time to go to sleep. We should check our posture, and perhaps try another chair.

What is more likely, especially in the case of dedicated people, is that we are not getting enough sleep and our Lord is telling us we should get more. We should do everything our Lord wants us to do. If we are not getting enough sleep, as well as enough recreation, time for friendship, and the like, the indication is that we are trying to do more than our Lord wants. That means we are getting in his way, doing things he wants to do himself or he wants others to do.

It may be, though, that our falling asleep is an escape. Twice in the Gospel, St. Luke tells us that the apostles fell asleep out of fear. It may be that we do not want to get too close to our Lord; we fear —we do not know what he might ask of us. Or it may be we are just not that interested in him: we are bored. The solution in either of these cases is to spend more time with the Gospels. We need to get to know the Lord better so that we will love him more, desire him more, trust him more.

How about walking while meditating?

In Centering Prayer, we want to be as free as we can to turn ourselves completely to the present God. Walking would demand a certain amount of attention to our own bodily activity, and to that extent it would detract from our freedom to be immediately to God. So it would be best not to walk during Centering Prayer, but to settle down.

In advanced Centering Prayer workshops, we have done some walking meditations between successive periods of centering. This afforded a helpful break between the periods of deep meditation and also allowed us to take some first gentle steps toward seeking to carry the centering over into activity.

In teaching others, is it good sometimes to give them a prayer word or at least to suggest one? Many who have learned meditation from an Eastern master have had a mantra given to them, and this has been very meaningful for them.

The author of *The Cloud* says we are to choose a meaningful word. Anyone who has a relationship with the Lord will have a word he uses habitually and spontaneously when addressing him. This word sums up for him the whole of his movement toward the Lord in faith and love. That is his prayer word. I find that most do not have any difficulty in choosing a word. By way of suggestion, the most I would do would be to quote from *The Cloud:* ". . . choose a short word rather than a long one. A one-syllable word such as 'God' or 'love' is best. But choose one that is meaningful to you."

If the person I were instructing should not yet have a consciously developed relation with our Lord, I would give him the name of Jesus. He would then be praying in the name of Jesus, he would realize that Jesus has a role to play in his coming to God, and as he listened to the Scriptures, he would come to find the full meaning of this saving Name.

By way of support, we might invite those we teach to share with us the word they have chosen and perhaps the reason why they have chosen it, and confirm them in their choice.

Is it all right to use a phrase like "Thy will be done"?

I would like to encourage pray-ers to stay with the directive of the author of *The Cloud* to choose a simple word. But in the things of the Spirit there is always freedom. I know a very beautiful nun who has chosen as her prayer word "Let go," and it is perfect for her. If one should choose a phrase, one should be particularly attentive to the advice of our author: "If your mind begins to intellectualize over the meaning and connotations of this little word, remind yourself that its value lies in its simplicity."

Is it all right to change my prayer word, or should I always use the same one?

Sometimes in the beginning, meditators like to try first one and then another word that is full of meaning for them. Certainly this is all right. It might also happen that on a particular occasion one would be drawn to a special word. "Where the Spirit is, there is freedom." But in general I think most people very quickly, if not immediately, discern what word is for them. And then it is best to stay with it. The word will grow in its facility to bring us quickly to the center and enable us to abide there in great quiet. Soon we will find that our word will spontaneously come in quiet moments and invite us to the center for a moment that will refresh.

What about the Gospel warning to avoid vain repetition?

The way we use the prayer word in Centering Prayer can hardly be considered vain repetition. We choose a meaningful word that expresses for us the whole of our movement into God in faith and love. And we use the word only in so far as it facilitates our abiding in deepest loving union with the Lord. Such repetition of the word can hardly be considered vain, or useless.

Sometimes I stop saying the prayer word. Is that all right?

We use the prayer word to the extent that it is useful and helps us to abide with the Lord. If that means using it constantly, fine; we use it constantly. If we do not need to use it, fine; we can let it go. We do not concern ourselves with whether or not we are using the word. It matters little. Our attention is to the Lord.

Sometimes when I am centering I begin to feel as though my hands and feet were no longer there. Is that OK?

We can indeed have feelings like that. We can have all sorts of feelings during our Prayer. Little matter. We treat them all the same. We apply the third rule any time we become aware of such feelings, and return to the presence of the Lord by means of our prayer word.

When we enter into Centering Prayer, our body is invited to rest deeply. The Lord wants to refresh it. The heartbeat and breathing usually slow down, our whole system grows quiet, and our extremities may well go to sleep. "I sleep, but my heart watches." It is good to make sure that the place we choose for our meditation is warm enough, or else, as our system quiets, we might become quite cold and be distracted and drawn out of our meditation by the cold.

Are there any writings on the physiological aspects of the Prayer of Centering?

So far as I know, there have not been any specific studies on the physiological effects of the Prayer of Centering. But I think Dr. Herbert Benson's general study on the effects of meditation of this type can legitimately be applied to the Prayer. The author of *The Cloud* in his own manner speaks of this in Chapter 54 of his treatise: "That contemplation graces a man with wisdom and poise and makes him attractive in body and spirit."

I notice that in the course of my meditation my head frequently falls forward and rests on my chest. What should I do?

I have had the same experience myself. If the back is straight and the head is perfectly balanced in place, it will remain erect when we lose consciousness of self in the Prayer. Otherwise the head will fall in one direction or another. When it does fall forward, it tends to put some strain on the neck, and this is what can call us out of the Prayer. If we become aware that our head has fallen forward, we gently straighten up and return to our Lord with our prayer word.

What if I feel itchy during the Prayer?

It is usually best just to attend to the itch and then return to the center with our prayer word.

I find at times that I come out of the Prayer feeling quite tired. I thought Centering Prayer was supposed to be restful.

If we do actually come out of the Prayer tired, then something is wrong. Perhaps we have not relaxed before beginning the Prayer. Or perhaps we are trying to achieve some state or fighting thoughts; in some way, we are failing to let go.

What might be happening, though, is that we are not actually feeling tired when we come out but are experiencing the effects of our system having profoundly quieted down during the meditation. It may take a little time for it to return to its normal state of activity. But when it does, we will be invigorated and probably feel more energetic from having gotten such a deep rest.

I think a lot of people expect something spectacular to happen. I mean, they really do. They think, when going to the center, getting in touch with God, that fireworks and lightning are going to fill the room. And when that doesn't happen, they think nothing has happened.

Father William Meninger, in his cassette talks on Centering Prayer (see Bibliography), speaks of the experience of Elijah, the prophet. Moses had encountered God on Mount Horeb in the midst of lightning and the roar of mighty thunder. But when the prophet Elijah was summoned to the same holy mountain, God was not to be found in the mighty wind, nor in the earthquake, nor in the fire, but in the quiet sound of a gentle breeze. In Centering Prayer, God is to be found in the inner silence.

An important thing is this: when we go to Centering Prayer, we should have no expectations whatsoever. We should come simply seeking God. If he wishes that there should be lightning and thunder, great experiences—fine! That's his business. If he wants us to abide in great quietness, that's great. If he wants us to be seemingly embroiled in a whole jumble of things, that's good too. Praised be his holy will! We do not come to Centering Prayer for inner peace, for experiences, for anything but for God himself. And if that is the case, we can be infallibly certain that it is he we will receive. And what more could we want? Everything else is secondary and inconsequential.

What about using images in Centering Prayer?

It is possible for us to center upon an image in prayer: a burning candle, an icon, the tabernacle door, the Sacred Host exposed (these are, of course, more than images). It is, in fact, impossible for us to pray at least initially without images, although we can move beyond them and contact God immediately as he is in himself. In Centering Prayer, we seek to employ what is perhaps the most apt image of God: a word. He has revealed himself, spoken to us in the Word. We fittingly respond to him in a word. But we seek to use a simple word and to use it as simply and purely as possible so that we can readily go beyond it and not get caught up in it as an image. The cloud and the concept of the center are used as secondary images, and these are apt images to use, for they are virtually imageless images, and do not readily invite us to get caught up in themselves, but leave us free to go beyond them to the Reality.

Is it better to read Scripture before, or after, doing Centering Prayer?

I think each one should have the courage to experiment a bit and discover which works best for him or her. Some find that reading Scripture before centering increases their desire and facilitates the Prayer. Others find that reading before centering tends to bring in a lot of concepts and images and makes the centering more difficult. On the other hand, the openness that the Centering Prayer engenders in them, the quietness, makes them more responsive to the Word of God when it is read after the Prayer. Others prefer to do their reading at another time, apart from the Prayer. Let each feel free to do whatever he or she finds best.

Is it better to meditate in a group, or alone?

Again, in practice this varies with the individual. Some find meditating with a group very supportive. There is no doubt that when we meditate together there are set up supportive currents of grace and even physical vibrations that are helpful to all in the group. However, some are by disposition more private persons. The presence of others makes them uneasy. Bodily sounds, even the gentle sound of another's breathing, invades their sense of quietness. They do better meditating by themselves. The accountability of gathering in a group to meditate periodically may be of such supportive value that it will override these considerations. With some patient and honest exploration and prudent consultation, each will find what is the best pattern for himself or herself.

How does Centering Prayer relate to charismatic prayer?

Charismatic prayer, as it has manifested itself and developed in the mainline churches, has tended to take on almost exclusively extroverted forms. But we should not forget that the Quaker sitting in silence is engaged in charismatic prayer.

When one is first drawn into charismatic prayer, it is usually a very affective prayer, full of very strong feelings and emotions and inviting very active expression. One should certainly move with this grace. But not infrequently it happens that, after a time, one feels drawn to more and more quiet and silence. This seems to happen to whole groups as they mature. It is at this point that instruction in the Centering Prayer method can be very supportive. In some areas, leaders of charismatic groups have made a conscious effort to learn how to teach Centering Prayer for this very reason, and have introduced into the format of the weekly program an opportunity, for those who wish, to learn Centering Prayer, to meditate together for a period, and to share their experiences and questions. This will usually take place in one of the small groups after the general prayer meeting. Thus the two forms of prayer are seen as complementary, and the one prayer program is supportive of both, according to the needs of each member.

In the few unfortunate instances in which charismatics have seen an opposition between Centering Prayer and charismatic prayer, it has usually been due to a lack of understanding of what precisely is meant by Centering Prayer and how it is founded on and is in fact an expression of an ancient Christian way of praying. Some open dialogue should easily clear away any misunderstanding.

Some leaders of charismatic prayer meetings have shared with me a certain personal concern. In their ministry they have seen members of their groups, sometimes persons who have been converted to the Lord a much shorter time than they, being drawn into the ways of contemplative prayer, while they themselves are still drawn to praise the Lord very actively in tongues and song. They wonder if they are missing something, if others are not passing them by. Of course it is possible that others are passing them by. God is the master of his gifts, and he need not give the most or the best to the leaders. But also, as we have said before, one's growth in love—and that is the essential growth in Christian life—is not to be correlated with the kind of prayer one practices. The important thing is to move with the Spirit and to pray as one can. But there may be something else here that an attentive discernment may bring out. Because of their particular call to ministry in leading the group and supporting those who are called to a very affective prayer, these men and women may be led to exercise on one level a very active form of prayer even while on a deeper level they are being nourished by a more contemplative type of prayer experience. While their tongues and voices sing forth God's praises, perhaps in unknown languages, their hearts rest deeply in God, nurtured by a very intimate union with him.

In any case, with wise discernment, each is to be encouraged to pray with all his or her heart in the way the Lord's Spirit is leading.

Finally, can you relate Centering Prayer to Liturgical Prayer?

According to ancient tradition, the night was divided into four watches, or nocturnes, and monks would watch in prayer throughout the night. Yet there were never more than two or three nocturnes in the liturgical Office. The fourth nocturne was always to be spent in contemplative prayer. The Office, with its psalms and lessons, is a school of prayer.

The Lord speaks to the soul and teaches it, and the man or woman who is participating in the Office begins to respond to this word, to this instruction, in the psalm prayers and in the collects.

But this response quite naturally flows over into the time when the Office is concluded and the church falls into silence. It is the time for contemplation. Centering Prayer can very well be used to prolong this prayerful response.

The Office feeds a contemplative prayer, evokes the deep desire for this kind of response and communion with the Lord. And this deep experience of the Lord can fill one with a great desire to burst forth in praise. *Benedictus Dominus Deus!* Lauds, morning song, follows upon the nocturnes. Vespers is often a fitting conclusion for an evening Centering Prayer. *Magnificat!*

Centering Prayer can very fittingly be integrated into the Eucharistic Liturgy. We are asked to begin this liturgical celebration by getting in touch with our own sinfulness, so that we might repent and draw mercy, be cleansed for the worthy offering of the holy Sacrifice. There is perhaps no better way to get in touch with our own sinfulness than to stand for a bit at the center in the immediate presence of the All-Holy. We spontaneously come out saying: "Lord, have mercy; Christ, have mercy; Lord, have mercy."

On another occasion, we might find it more fitting to wait until we have been cleansed by the absolution of the celebrant. We can then more worthily center upon the wonder of our God of mercy and come forth in the joyful hymn of praise: "Glory to God in the highest. . . ." Centering can also find a place before the readings, to prepare a quiet and receptive mind and heart for the Word, or after them, in response.

Some like to use the pause after receiving Holy Communion to center. I find myself drawn at this time to center on the physical presence of our Lord Jesus in the Eucharist, rather than on the spiritual presence at the ground of my being. But perhaps this is where the Eucharistic Lord tends to lead us.

The Liturgy nourishes Centering Prayer and evokes an ever greater desire to enter into this experience. The experience of Centering Prayer in its turn fills us with desire to receive more fully the enlightenment and instruction of the Liturgy and to enter into its movements of repentance, prayer, thanksgiving, and praise. They are both part of an integral Christian life, which must always be a life of prayer.

XIV

MARY, AT THE HEART OF THINGS

It is not easy for us to capture an image of that simple and simply lovely maiden whom heaven summoned to the most exalted service that a human person could fulfill: that of mothering God himself. We of America are fortunate in being the recipients of that miraculous image that hid beneath the roses on Fray Juan's cloak and today is enshrined in the basilica at Guadalupe, near Mexico City. It captures, perhaps more closely than any other picture we have, something of the beauty of the maiden of Nazareth. And yet it can only hint in the most distant sort of way at the beauty of that person, that beautiful young girl—dare we call her that? So she certainly appears to our eyes even though she was mothering—what a ponderous mystery was laid upon her heart!

Again and again the divinely inspired writer repeats that refrain: "She pondered all these things in her heart." The shepherds came and spoke of hosts of heavenly choirs, of a king of the house of David, of a savior who would save his people. And then there was that holy old man, Simeon. . . . The whole longing of Israel, the longing she had begun to enter into, was summed up in his person. And now he spoke of fulfillment and savior and sign and discernment and rejection and—what was that?—a sword for her own heart! And Anna—a woman's word seemed to touch even closer.

And the mystery of those three days—foreshadowing another three days when she would well know the sword. The fifth mystery of the rosary follows upon the fourth. To the temple, a woman filled with wonder, like every Jewish mother before, but with an unprecedented fullness and meaning, brought her First-born and offered him back to the Giver of life, Yahweh, his God and—oh, so mysteriously—his Father! He was ransomed with the ransom of the poor, not even thirty pieces of silver.

The event slipped into the background. Life moved on, so filled with the commonplace after the strange Egyptian interlude, which in fact was perhaps not so strange to a people close to their nomadic ancestors, a people that had so often known exile. Were there Nazareth days when the maiden all but forgot who her Son was, and who she was, and how completely he belonged to his Father? In any case, when he was suddenly "about his Father's business," it was a shock. And his declaration of the fact made it no more intelligible.

We, too, in times of grace make our offering of all to the Father. And then we go about our daily doings, all but forgetting what we have done. And then comes the day when the Father lays claim to what is his. And we, too, are shocked, and seek, and cry out: Why have you done this to us?

And Mary pondered all this in her heart.

One modern translation has rendered this phrase: And she pondered all this in her mind. That is very much our mind-set. When we ponder, we think things over. But that is not what the Scriptures tell us Mary did. She pondered them in her heart. That is the way her people meditated. And that is the way the monks have traditionally meditated. For meditation did not mean thinking something over, dissecting it, analyzing and synthesizing and trying to come to conclusions. Nor did it mean a great workout for the imagination. Rather, it meant just letting the fact of revelation quietly rehearse itself in the mind and press upon the heart. It was weighed in the heart, until its weight gave direction to the heart. And the heart responded to the reality.

Centering Prayer is a prayer of the heart. The "meaningful word," summing up a response to a revelation of personal love, expressed more fully in the opening movement of the Prayer, quietly gives direction to the heart, so that it might flow according to its own true nature in the current of the fullness of Divine Love. When we come to know this Prayer, this reality that is prayer, then we come to know from within as our own that magnificent hymn of our virgin Mother. Our whole being proclaims it:

> My soul proclaims the greatness of the Lord
>   and my spirit exults in God my savior;
> because he has looked on his lowly servant.
>
> For the Almighty has done great things for me.
>   Holy is his name,
> and his mercy reaches from age to age
>   to those who fear him.

Right from the very start, this chosen virgin was not taken up with her own dignity, not taken up with her own fears. She was a woman of loving service, of serving love. A need was made known to her and she responded, and at great cost. The excitement, the fears, the wonder of a first pregnancy, the anxieties of a mystified fiancé, the dangers, the fatigues of a long journey to the hill country, did not hold her back. It was not a great spiritual mission she saw for herself; she went only to offer the most humble sort of service. But she knew who dwelt within. She was full with God because she was totally open to God, a complete "yes" to his demanding love. And so she brought God Christ, she brought grace and joy, she brought the Holy Spirit.

And in ministering to others, she was ministered unto. Whenever the Lord calls upon us to serve others, it is in his most merciful and sublime design that we who serve are to be the greatest recipients of our service. Christ died for us and for our salvation, but none receives such glory from his glorious death as does he. Mary came to serve and minister, but she herself was ministered unto. She received a confirmation of her own grace. God responded to Mary's very human need. He gave her an older woman who was going through, as much as any woman ever could, what Mary herself was experiencing—not just motherhood, but a mysterious spiritual motherhood coming about by an intervention from heaven itself. How good it was that someone else knew and understood!

Mary received affirmation and praise: praise not only for the objectively wonderful thing that the Lord had done for her in making her the mother of the Lord himself, but for her subjective response to it, for her belief. The old woman who had lived for months now with a mute husband could very well appreciate this young woman's faith. Her own must have known its challenge. And Mary accepted the praise. She accepted reality. She accepted the praise and referred it according to reality. "He that is mighty has done great things for me." Not just her pregnancy, but also her faith, was a gift.

One of my confreres shared this story with me: His little niece used to go to Mass each Sunday with her mother and father, brothers and sisters. As a little one, she was full of questions, and her mother sought to find answers that would satisfy the little inquirer and help her grow in her faith. The little girl pointed up to the stained-glass windows with their many saintly figures and asked: "Who are they?" "They are the saints," her mother replied. Some time later, when the child was in nursery school, Sister asked, "Who are the saints?" A little hand shot up. "Well," said Sister, "who are the saints?" With excited pride the little one responded, "They are the ones who let God's light shine through."

Mary let God's light shine through: He that is mighty has done great things for me, and holy is his name.

And Mary went on to prophesy in truth: "Every generation shall call me blessed." Ever since the day when a voice rose from the crowd and declared: "Blessed is the womb that bore you and the breasts that fed you," lips have not ceased to repeat:

> Hail, Mary, full of grace,
>   the Lord is with you.
> Blessed are you among women. . . .

And equally true is her prophecy: "His mercy is from generation unto generation to those who fear him." Any one of us who opens to God and allows him the space, the time in which to manifest himself and his sustaining, creative presence within, will be a bearer of God, of grace, of Spirit to each one to whom we come in service, and in serving we ourselves will be ministered unto, affirmed, confirmed, called forth to an ever greater fullness and sense of life and love.

Today (March 19) is the feast of St. Joseph. In his homily at Mass this morning, Father Abbot spoke of the "loss of Mary." I think this can say a number of things to us.

Often, those who have had a special, tender devotion to Mary, sometimes from childhood and a mother's knee, in the first days of a renewed Christian life suffer a loss of Mary. From being quite central and as it were universally present, lovingly mothering us and calling forth a delicious devotion—our Life, our Sweetness, and our Hope—Mary seems to fade from the picture. The Mother turns us toward her Son, the Center of her own life and its full meaning.

There is a not uncommon pattern: First Mary mothers the tender Christian till he or she is mature enough to enter into a real friendship with her Son. The Son in turn leads his friend and brother or sister to his Father. The Father with the Son animates the lover's life with their Spirit. The beloved finds himself within the Trinity, and there discovers again Mary at the heart of the Trinity's love, a pervading presence in her universal mothering mediation. And then we know more truly that she is life, sweetness, hope. We should expect this loss, this cutting of spiritual apron strings, as we break away from the supportive home of sensible consolation and go out into the night of faith. But when we truly come home, Mary will be very much there.

But there is another lesson in this "loss of Mary." Joseph, the just one, the faithful, the lover of Mary, had to give her up in order to truly possess her as wife and beloved in the Lord. How hard it must have been! Who in all of God's creation could have been more difficult to give up than this fairest daughter of God? Yet the challenging question thrust itself upon this just man, Joseph: Do you love me more than her? Joseph perhaps struggled long and hard over the decision, or rather to discern if the question was really being asked. When the question became clear, his answer was heroic. It merited an angelic visit.

In today's Mass the first reading was of the prophetic foreshadowing of this. Abraham, too, was asked, but this time it was of a son: Abraham, do you love me more than him? And Abraham trekked to Horeb, fire and sword in hand. And his existential profession of love also merited the visit of a staying angel.

Mary is a wonderful mother and model, a caring support and presence. Yet as we go to the center, we must leave even her behind. Some like to prefix their Centering Prayer with a Hail Mary to acknowledge her universal mediation and persisting presence. Yet as we enter into the center and pass beyond the veil in faith, . we must leave all thought of the Virgin behind and enter in and stand, as it were, alone and naked before our God. We must leave behind our Life, our Sweetness, and our Hope. We must leave behind everything. Mary had to let go even of Christ, at least in his sensible and physical presence, to hold him only in faith. And we, too, must needs say with St. Paul: "We knew him once in the flesh, but we know him so no more." But if we can fully imitate the Woman of Faith, and not waver in our hearts, when the seemingly long Holy Saturday of this life of faith is finally over, the all too quickly passing experiences of the Taboric Light will give way to the vision of the Source. And there, in the heart of the Trinity, at the right of him who sits upon his Father's throne and promised we would share his throne, we will find again, in all her glory, our Life, our Sweetness and our Hope. William of Saint Thierry wrote:

> And such is the astounding generosity of the Creator to the creature: the great grace, the unknowable goodness, the devout confidence of the creature for the Creator, the tender approach, the tenderness of a good conscience, that man somehow finds himself in their midst, in the embrace and kiss of the Father and Son, that is, in the Holy Spirit. And he is united to God by that charity whereby the Father and the Son are one. He is made holy in him who is the holiness of both. The sense of this good and the tenderness of this experience, as great as it can be in this miserable and deceptive life, although it is not now full, is yet a true and truly blessed life! (*Mirror of Faith*, 17)

If it is so now, how will it be then! If it is so for us, how will it be for the all-faithful, totally loving, sinless One!

Mary, our model in centering, teaches us how to leave even our model behind. Mary, our model, in her unending, motherly love and caring, shows us the way to live a centered life, a life of serving love, the fruit of Centering Prayer. Mary, our model, in her glory in the heart of the Trinity, is a sign and a pledge of the consummation of our fidelity to the Prayer.

We cannot adequately praise this most holy and glorious Virgin. Yet there is no way in which we can better praise her and please her than by living centered lives and letting the fruits of Centering Prayer blossom forth in our lives, to the glory of her Son, with whom we are one, and in whose Spirit we are one with him in a total "yes" to the Father.

To the most holy and blessed, glorious and exalted Trinity be all honor and glory, now and forever!

EPILOGUE: DREAM—OR VISION?

I have a dream. I see all the earth in peace, the whole human family living together, sharing the fruits of creation and the joy that comes from the good things of our planet and beyond. And this peace and joy, a universal compassion, flows within and out of the worldwide Christian family. Our brothers and sisters of other faiths, all people of good will, exclaim: "Blessed are the peacemakers, for they are the children of God." And each one of us Christians does indeed know, by personal experience, that he or she is a much-loved child of God. Our lives are filled with love and security, joy and peace. Each one is in touch with his or her own contemplative dimension. Busy days flow out of a deep center. Space is found, time set apart, to enjoy a Father's intimate loving presence and to let him enjoy us.

It began in the seminaries and houses of formation for religious. True spiritual fathers and mothers evoked a vision, showed a way. And those who came forth to minister to God's people were men and women who lived out of the center, who were constantly in touch with the loving and nurturing Presence of God in all. They knew the Father well and were able with and in Christ to show others the Father.

On every campus there were those in ministry, spiritual fathers and mothers, who radiated joy and enthusiasm, who reflected and shared a great vision, a vision worthy of the gift of one's life. They knew how to open the way for the students by teaching them the ways of Christian meditation, so that the young men and women were able themselves to experience the Father's love and be formed by his Spirit according to the mind and heart of Christ. The campuses were dotted with meditation rooms where the busy students could go apart for a while and, in a supportive environment, with others, find moments of deep grounding so that their vitally active lives could flow out of the true Source. And each Christian came to sense his anointing in Christ, his call, his mission among the people of God and the whole human family.

Back home in the parish it was not different. The parish priest had his apostolic assistants, those whom he had the joy of especially calling forth, in whose lives he experienced the generativity of his spiritual paternity. And together they opened out to all the fellow members of their parish community the ways of deeper prayer, of personal experience of the Father's ever-present creative and sustaining love. There were the parish meditation groups in which especially the singles, the separated, all the lonely, could experience true belonging, true caring, true community. Each home had its own program, its rhythm of meditation. And as each family sat together, centering, together in the Lord, even the littlest ones, held in loving arms or resting in their bassinets, experienced enfolding currents of love that they would never forget, that they would never want to be absent from their lives.

Schools began their days with a common experience of the Source of all knowledge. Wherever Christians gathered, they first sought to experience their deep unity by going to the center together. No communal prayer service, celebration, or liturgy was without its significant moments of silence when all, experienced in finding God in the center, quickly entered into the familiar depths.

How could there not be peace in such communities? How could such communities not radiate peace?

And I see especially the retirement homes, the rest homes, the communities of senior citizens, the infirmaries where retired priests and religious enter into the last phase of their vocation. For all of these, life has acquired a new and rich significance. They have become aware of their call to enter more and more deeply into the contemplative heart of the whole Christ and to be a part of that source from which currents of grace, love, and life flow out upon their families: their children, their grandchildren, and their great-grandchildren, their religious families, the parish families they once so selflessly served. How joyful and meaningful are the declining years of these men and women who have grown into truest wisdom as they ever deepen their contact with the vital new currents that flow among God's children and ever mother the Christ life in them!

Dream—or vision? Is it realistic? If each one who has already learned a way to daily touch the Lord, to ground his or her life at the Source, teaches one other and sends forth that other to teach yet another, will not the paths to peace be multiplied? But why should we not bear fruit thirtyfold, sixtyfold, a hundredfold?

It is difficult to see, in our frenetic society, how we can keep from losing ourselves and being totally dissipated and fragmented if we do not get in touch with our deeper selves, if we are not in touch with the ground of our being and find our true selves in that unifying Source of Being.

We have been commanded, and it is in fact a law of our very being, that we are to love others even as we love ourselves. If we experience in our own selves the need, the value, and the joy of being in touch with the contemplative dimension of our lives, then is it not incumbent upon us to seek to make this possible also for others? "Freely have you received, freely must you give."

A dream can become a vision when it is shared and shared effectively. Let us begin, then, to change a dream into a vision. For I think ultimately it is a glimmer of the dream of a God who in his goodness beyond comprehension has given us the dignity of the responsibility of changing his dream into a living reality. We should not let the magnitude of the task deter us from doing our little bit. Our ripple can become a wave. He who is our Master, the Teacher of the Way, began with a few poor neighbors—not the brightest. But he gave them what he had, as best he could—it was a discouraging experience that evoked salty tears of disappointment—and then he called upon the Father to send the Spirit. And it went on from there.

We began this book by considering the role of the Spirit in helping us to penetrate the dream of God—what eye has not seen, nor ear heard, what is beyond the conception of the human mind—so that it might become the actual vision of our own lives. God has revealed this to us through the Spirit. Now it is time to seek that, through us, by the working of the same Spirit of Love who dwells in us, this vision might be imparted to others.

There is no greater gift we can give people than to open out to them the way by which they can come to experience most intimately and constantly how much they are loved by God.

SELECTED BIBLIOGRAPHY

Books

Anonymous. *The Cloud of Unknowing and The Book of Privy Counseling*, ed. W. Johnston (Garden City, NY: Doubleday, 1973).

Abhishiktananda (Fr. Henri Le Saux, O.S.B.). *Prayer* (Philadelphia: Westminster Press, 1973).

Benson, Herbert. *Relaxation Response* (New York: William Morrow, 1975).

Bloom, Anthony. *Beginning to Pray* (New York: Paulist Press, 1971).

———. *Living Prayer* (Springfield, IL: Templegate, 1966).

Chariton of Valamo. *The Art of Prayer* (London: Faber & Faber, 1966).

Evagrius Ponticus. *Praktikos. Chapters on Prayer* (Spencer, MA: Cistercian Publications, 1970).

Griffiths, Bede. *Return to the Center* (Springfield, IL: Templegate, 1976).

Hausherr, Ireneé. *The Name of Jesus* (Kalamazoo, MI: Cistercian Publications, 1978).

Higgins, John J. *Thomas Merton on Prayer* (Garden City, NY: Doubleday, 1972).

Hodgson, Phyllis, ed. *Deonise Hid Divinite and other Treatises on Contemplative Prayer Related to The Cloud of Unknowing* (London: Oxford University Press, 1958).

John of the Cross. *The Collected Works* (Washington, DC: I.C.S. Publications, 1973).

Johnston, William. *The Inner Eye of Love* (San Francisco: Harper & Row, 1978).

———. *The Mysticism of The Cloud of Unknowing* (St. Meinrad, IN: Abbey Press, 1975).

———. *Silent Music* (New York: Harper & Row, 1974).

———. *The Stillpoint* (New York: Fordham University Press, 1970).

Kadloubovsky, E.; and Palmer, G. E. H., eds. *Early Fathers from the Philokalia* (London: Faber & Faber, 1954).

———. *Writings from the Philokalia on Prayer of the Heart* (London: Faber & Faber, 1951).

Keating, Thomas, et al. *Finding Grace at the Center* (Still River, MA: St. Bede Press, 1978).

Lawrence, Brother. *Practice of the Presence of God* (Springfield, IL: Templegate, 1974).

Louf, André. *Teach Us to Pray* (New York: Paulist Press, 1978).

Maloney, George. *Inward Stillness* (Denville, NJ: Dimension Books, 1976).

Merton, Thomas. *The Climate of Monastic Prayer* (Kalamazoo, MI: Cistercian Publications, 1969).

———. *Contemplative Prayer* (Garden City, NY: Doubleday, 1971).

———. *The New Man* (New York: Farrar, Straus & Giroux, 1961).

Naranjo, C.; and Ornstein, R. E. *On the Psychology of Meditation* (New York: The Viking Press, 1971).

Pennington, M. Basil. *Daily We Touch Him* (Garden City, NY: Doubleday, 1977).

———. *In Search of True Wisdom* (Garden City, NY: Doubleday, 1979).

Richards, M. C. *Centering in Pottery, Poetry and the Person* (Middletown, CT: Wesleyan University Press, 1964).

Teresa of Avila. *Interior Castle* (Garden City, NY: Doubleday, 1961).

———. *The Way of Perfection* (Garden City, NY: Doubleday, 1964).

William of Saint Thierry. *On Contemplating God, Prayer, Meditations* (Kalamazoo, MI: Cistercian Publications, 1977).

Articles

Bernier, Paul. "Conversation with Basil Pennington," *Emmanuel* 85(1979): 69–86.

Clark, Thomas. "Finding Grace at the Center," *The Way* 17(1977): 12–22.

Gilles, Anthony E. "Three Modes of Meditation," *America* 139(1978): 52–54.

Keating, Thomas. "Contemplative Prayer in the Christian Tradition," *America* 138(1978): 278–81.

———. "Cultivating the Centering Prayer," *Review for Religious* 37(1978): 10–15.

———. "Meditative Prayer," *Today's Catholic Teacher* 12, no. 5 (Feb. 1979): 32–33.

Llewelyn, Robert. "The Positive Role of Distractions in Prayer," *Fairacres Chronicle* 8, no. 2 (Summer 1975): 22–29.

Main, John. "Prayer in the Tradition of John Cassian," *Cistercian Studies* 12(1977): 184–90, 272–81; 13(1978): 75–83.

Nouwen, Henri. "Unceasing Prayer," *America* 139(1978): 46–51.

Pennington, M. Basil. "Centering Prayer: the Christian Privilege," *Emmanuel* 85(1979): 61–68.

———. "Centering Prayer—Prayer of Quiet," *Review for Religious* 35(1976): 651–62.

———. "Listening to the Fathers," *Spiritual Life* 24(1978): 12–17.

———. "T M and Christian Prayer," *Pastoral Life* 25(1976): 9–16.

Cassettes

Keating, Thomas. "Contemplative Prayer in the Christian Tradition. Historical Insights" (Spencer, MA: St. Joseph's Abbey).

Main, John. "Christian Meditation: Our Oldest and Newest Form of Prayer" (Kansas City, MO: NCR Cassettes).

Meninger, William. "Contemplative Prayer" (Spencer, MA: St. Joseph's Abbey).

Pennington, M. Basil. "A Centered Life: A Practical Course on Centering Prayer and Its Place in Our Lives" (Kansas City, MO: NCR Cassettes).